DATE DUE

NO 11 '93			
MY 13 '94			
DE 23 '94			
MY 12 '95			
DE 15 '99			
DE 18 03			
AG 5 08			

THE
BEST JOBS
IN AMERICA

FOR PARENTS
WHO WANT
CAREERS
AND TIME FOR
CHILDREN TOO

THE
BEST JOBS
IN AMERICA

FOR PARENTS WHO WANT CAREERS AND TIME FOR CHILDREN TOO

SUSAN BACON DYNERMAN

LYNN O'ROURKE HAYES

RAWSON ASSOCIATES
NEW YORK

COLLIER MACMILLAN CANADA
TORONTO

MAXWELL MACMILLAN INTERNATIONAL
NEW YORK   OXFORD   SINGAPORE   SYDNEY

HD5109.2.U5 D95 1991
Dynerman, Susan Bacon, 1952
The best jobs in America fo
parents who want careers an
time for children too

ier Macmillan Canada, Inc.
) Eglinton Avenue East
: 200
Mills, Ontario M3C 3N1

Library of Congress Cataloging-in-Publication Data

Dynerman, Susan Bacon, 1952–
   The best jobs in America for parents who want careers—and time for children too
/ Susan Bacon Dynerman, Lynn O'Rourke Hayes
       p.   cm.
   Includes bibliographical references and index.
   ISBN 0-89256-351-6 (hardcover)
   1. Hours of labor, Flexible—United States.   2. Part-time
employment—United States.   3. Dual career families—United States.
4. Working mothers—United States—Time management.   5. Child care
services—United States.   6. Work and family—United States.
I. Hayes, Lynn O'Rourke, 1955–   II. Title.
HD5109.2.U5H39   1991
331.7′02′024043—dc20   90-46058
                                                                       CIP

Designed by Stanley S. Drate, Folio Graphics
Produced by Rapid Transcript, a division of March Tenth, Inc.

Names of many people quoted in the text have been changed to protect their privacy.

Macmillan books are available at special discounts for bulk purchases for sales
promotions, premiums, fund-raising, or educational use. For details, contact:

                    Special Sales Director
                    Macmillan Publishing Company
                    866 Third Avenue
                    New York, NY 10022

10   9   8   7   6   5   4   3   2   1

Printed in the United States of America

To my mother and father,
Joan and Al Bacon
—S.B.D.

To my husband, Peter Madison Hayes
—L.O.H.

CONTENTS

Acknowledgments   ix

PART I
Flexible Jobs:
Changing the Way We Work

1 The Quiet Revolution   *3*

2 The Changing Needs of a Changing
Work Force   *17*

3 From the Inside Out: Reshaping the
Workplace   *34*

4 Leaders in Flexibility   *51*

5 Flexibility, Equality, Maternity: Where to
from Here?   *67*

PART II

How to Get
the Flexible Job You Want

6 Making the Flexible Choice   *93*

7 The Negotiating Table   *109*

8 Ten Successful Job Strategies   *131*

9 On the Job: Making Flexibility Work   *154*

10 Things You Should Know About Job
Flexibility   *174*

PART III

Resources for Your Job Search

Corporate Policy Guide   *189*

The Flexible Options: A Glossary   *209*

Guide to Resources   *213*

Bibliography   *231*

Index   *235*

ACKNOWLEDGMENTS

We talked to hundreds of people to put together this book. Our thanks to the parents who shared their experiences and gave their time—often at odd hours of the night—for no reason other than an intense interest in this subject. And thanks also to the reporters and research assistants who provided the leads we needed to get a sense of what was happening all over the country—Miriam Pepper, Joni Blackman, Tara Weingarten, Linda DiPietro, Lindy Voss, Mike Mason, Ryan Renner, and Steve Sawicki, who contacted scores of companies for the section on corporate policies.

A handful of researchers and work/family consultants took time to share their insights with us—Arlene Johnson, Graham Staines, Fran Rodgers, Gil Gordon, Kathleen Christensen, Christine Scordato, Karen Gaertner, and Stanley Nollen. Our special thanks to Ellen Galinsky, Judy David, and the people at the Families and Work Institute in New York for inviting us to review a massive amount of data on corporate policies collected for their Corporate Reference Guide. To Diane Ingraham, our appreciation for translating tapes into impeccable manuscripts and bringing order to chaos. And to the three people who believed in this project and guided it to completion—Heide Lange, Grace Shaw, and Eleanor Rawson.

Thanks to my friends and family who provided advice, read manuscripts, made impromptu trips to the library, sent clippings, and gave us leads—Pat Sachs, Bunny Goldstein, Ann Hoenigswald, Jack Greenberg, and above all, my sister, Abby Bacon. My deep appreciation to Tim Benford and Elizabeth Wilson, who helped with this project when we needed it most—before we had an agent or a publisher; without those two people, this book might not exist.

I couldn't ask for a more supportive family. My parents came to Washington and ran my house when I, predictably, came down with the flu at deadline time. They took care of me and my family, and made sure the manuscript got in the mail. Thanks to my husband, Alan, and sons, Max and Alex, who inspire and motivate and are a constant source of joy. To Arcelia Aguilar, who took care of Max so I could write this book, and Calvin Turley, who took care of Alex.

Finally, my thanks to Bob Towery, the publisher who gave me not only my first writing job, but my first flexible job.

—S.B.D.

I must begin by expressing my deepest gratitude to my husband, Peter Hayes, without whom I couldn't have written the first word. His good-natured patience, support, advice, and encouragement kept me going when juggling the demands of three children, a flexible job, and a book project seemed overwhelming.

Without the extraordinary personal and professional support of Jerry Petitt, the president of Choice Hotels International, this book would not have been conceived. His early support of job-sharing and his ongoing willingness to provide flexibility has allowed me to combine a career with the most important job I'll ever have—motherhood. His own ability to balance work and family is in itself an inspiration.

A special thanks to Bob Hazard, Choice's chairman, for his support of my flexible schedule. For him, it hasn't been easy. Thanks also to Tony Rothwell for his early participation.

I am indebted to Bonnie Groover, Wendy Grant, and Patrice Heath for their good-spirited assistance. Also thanks to Andrea Butler, Scott Baum, and Eileen Griffin.

For the almost daily encouragement and wholehearted support received from my dearest friends Wendy Black and Betsy Bromberg I am deeply grateful. They were terrific.

Help and encouragement came in special and important ways from Mike O'Rourke, Sarah Hayes, Tim Benford, Nancy Hayes, Jan Smith, Rebecca Clay, Kathleen Mathews, Jennifer Cunningham, and BBBHKR.

Two others deserve a special mention: I am deeply indebted to Bob Lawrence, a wonderful friend, father, and professional whose wise counsel and warm sense of humor added focus to my effort. I am also deeply grateful to Paula Panich for taking time to read through the manuscript and offer thoughtful advice. Her steady support has been a constant source of inspiration.

A very special thank-you to my parents. My father, Harry O'Rourke, taught me early on never to give up. He was never far away during this project. My mother, Ann O'Rourke, taught me patience and the meaning of unconditional love. I miss her friendship daily.

Finally, thanks to my three magnificent sons, Benjamin, Alexander, and Theodore. Each in his own way inspired me to write this book.

—L.O.H.

PART
I

FLEXIBLE
JOBS:

Changing the
Way We Work

1

THE QUIET
REVOLUTION

THREE WOMEN

Cathy Crawford is thirty-five years old. She's in management-level recruiting at Hewlett-Packard's California headquarters. Her title, which itself reads like a classified ad, is Experienced Recruiting Programs Manager in Human Resource Staffing. Her hours? She works twenty hours a week—two full days plus a half-day of meetings.

Articulate and confident, she comfortably fits the image of a young, career-minded woman on the way up in a major U.S. corporation. She spent ten years at the division level. By thirty-three, she'd hit middle management, supervising ten people at a California division office.

"I was very dedicated. I worked long hours and weekends. Working full-time, that's the only way I could operate and meet the standards I set for myself," says Crawford. When, at thirty-three, she and her husband, Dave, adopted their first child, she knew something had to give. Dave is a pilot, absent about 50 percent of the time. "I couldn't visualize myself being Supermom in some fantasy world, given that I would essentially be a single mom half of the month. And," she adds, "I really wanted to be a part of my child's life."

"When I went on leave, I didn't know what I was going to do. I tried to get my hands on all the information I could about 'what happens if I quit work or take a long leave.' It was like a phobia. I was really very upset about it," says Crawford, who now has two children under the age of two. "I was afraid if I did get off track, if I took some time off, I'd be out. I felt like I'd be giving up what it took me so long to attain." For Crawford, a part-time slot was a chance to keep her foot in the door.

Sarah Clarke lives in Washington, D.C., city of the eighty-hour work week, where the children of high-powered professionals are as likely to be on the fast track as their parents. With a master's degree in international relations from The Fletcher School, Clarke is an expert in terrorism and crisis management at a Washington think tank. In 1982, after her first child was born, she converted a full-time job into a thirty-hour-a-week position. Seven years and three pregnancies later, Clarke has earned several promotions, moving to the level of research fellow.

She's not standing still, but she's not on the fast track either. Her salary, measured against the standards of Washington's power elite, is low at $30,000 a year. But for a part-time job, it's more than respectable and, considering that her field tops out at $55,000 for a full-timer, it's even competitive. Although her work week often stretches to thirty-five hours, she imposes restraints on herself: "I could have taken project directorships. My boss travels and I don't," she says. "I keep putting the brakes on myself. A few weeks ago, I was offered the chance to go to a major conference. I didn't go. Or they'll say, 'Let's fly to New York and pitch this project,' and I have to say no."

The lives of her children, who range in age from four to seven, are filled with extracurricular activities—art, dance, piano lessons. Her four-year-old is taking Orff music lessons; her seven-year-old is enrolled in a Japanese language immersion program. She clearly has high expectations for her kids as well as for herself. "I am the liaison with the school, the doctor, the dentist. I handle the extracurricular activities, the Halloween parade, scheduling car pools, and baking cookies." That's not a role she could play, she feels, while working full-time. "I think the closest I've come to a nervous breakdown was trying to be a perfect mother and a perfect employee. I was a perfect nothing."

Glenda Elkins is forty-one. Her round, freckled face masks a quick, dry wit and underlying cynicism. Her style is loose and relaxed. She wears blue jeans to work. Elkins has, by any standards, paid her dues. She's been through two marriages and supported her family through both, while raising two children. When she was still in her early thirties, she reached the top of her field in Memphis, Tennessee. As copy chief for a major regional ad agency, she played the role of creative director, overseeing the entire art and copywriting departments.

Elkins worked full-time until her sons were eleven and thirteen. Then, her second marriage dissolving and feeling dead-ended in the agency business, she went out on her own. "I left with the intent of freelancing, but that was really scary to me. I had two kids and needed insurance and the kind of security you don't get as a freelance writer," she says. After less than a year on her own, she got a call from another Memphis agency, a competitor of her long-time employer. They offered her a part-time job, replacing a full-time copywriter, taking on his salary and all his projects, but operating on a three-day work week. She accepted.

Explains Elkins: "There's a real shortage of writers in Memphis and they needed someone who had experience." The agency pays her $35,000 a year for the three days' work and she earns additional pay on a daily basis if she puts in more time. "They couldn't have paid the fifty-thousand it would have taken to get a senior writer. This way, they get a senior writer at a junior salary. I've picked up all his accounts and the accounts of another writer who has since left. I can handle twice the load of a midrange copywriter with three or four years of experience. I'm fast and I'm good."

For Elkins, flexibility means college tuition for the kids, a lifestyle change, security for her future. "In my original job, I was making fifty thousand dollars a year plus a car and bonuses. I knew I might get a five-thousand-dollar raise a year, but that isn't a lot of money. I felt like I'd topped out. I was going to have to make thirty thousand more than I was making to change my standard of living and send the kids to school." The extra two days a week give her time to write. She's already into her second book—one that she hopes will earn her the income she needs to build for her children's future.

On the face of it, these three women have little in common. They live in different worlds. Their career goals, their values, their attitudes about work and family are quite different. But they're representative of the kind of people we encountered while researching this book. They're smart, motivated, talented, and dedicated to their work—the kind of people who make good employees. They've all confronted the thorny issue of how to balance their personal and professional goals against the desire to raise a family. And, in weighing work and family, they have fashioned their own, unique arrangements.

They are pioneers, participants in a quiet revolution under way in the American workplace. As people holding professional and management-level jobs that are less than full-time, Crawford, Elkins, and Clarke are no longer anomalies. We found their counterparts everywhere—in major corporations, government jobs, small businesses; in education, publishing, broadcasting, and health care. We found professionals—doctors, lawyers, teachers, and architects—who put in less than full-time hours. We found part-timers in supervisory and management positions.

We also saw genuine signs of change. Some companies are not just allowing flexibility, they're promoting it in employee newsletters and personnel brochures, through training programs and job posting. Some even have on-site consultants to guide employees through the process of developing and negotiating more flexibility.

Two things seem to be going on simultaneously, and even independently. On the one hand, these top performers have been quietly negotiating for more flexibility. On the other hand, more and more American employers are coming around to the view that if they don't offer flexible options they're going to lose talented people—men and women—to outmoded styles of work. "It's ironic, isn't it?" says Arlene Johnson, senior research associate at the Conference Board's Work and Family Information Center in New York. "For a long time, flexible work hours, parental leave, child care—these issues were seen as being pushed by women to enable them to enter the work force. Now the tables are turned. They're being used by corporations to lure women in and to keep them there."

This book is about the kinds of flexible careers that exist today—job-sharing, flexible schedules, part-time careers, and extended parental leaves. Obviously, not all working parents can afford to reduce their hours and incomes, so we'll look at other corporate strategies that may help working parents— policies like care for sick children, flextime, personal time off, and part-time return options following maternity leave. Part I is about the pace of these changes: the kinds of jobs that exist and where we found them. Part II covers how to negotiate and manage these new, more flexible positions. Part III provides a guide to resources, including profiles of twenty-five flexible companies and their policies.

In the course of our research, we interviewed one hundred women and men who have achieved a degree of flexibility in jobs that have not historically been considered flexible; in other words, we didn't talk to self-employed people or salespeople or real estate agents. We gathered data on more than one hundred employers in an effort to determine the depth of the changes under way. What we found was, in some respects, quite exciting. A surprising number of companies offer a certain amount of flexibility and many more are beginning to look at flexible options. Most important, flexibility is on the corporate agenda, a first step toward legitimizing such arrangements. The best news: these individually negotiated arrangements are not only widespread; they seem to be *working*—from both the employee's perspective and the employer's. They are models for a change that is sorely needed to make working parents full partners in the American economy.

WHY WE WROTE THIS BOOK

Lynn and I, Susan, began this project in 1988, when we were sharing a job as director of communications for a major hotel company. It seemed as if every time someone asked us what we did, not an uncommon question in our hometown of Washington, D.C., we were greeted with a barrage of questions. How did you do it? How much do you work? Is it working? How unusual is it? Or, more to the point, How can I get such a job? We couldn't help but wonder how widespread job-sharing had become and how much interest there was in such alternative arrangements.

We noticed something else going on around us—at work and at home. We realized that we were the highest-ranking women with young children at our company's headquarters. Running down the list of women at the director level or above, we ticked off the names of single women, married women without children, and a handful of women with teenagers at home. But not one woman with children under ten was working at the management level. Then, we looked around us. We had five friends and neighbors with new babies. The mothers included a lawyer, an editor, an executive, a writer, and a full-time mother. Of the five, only one—the executive—was going back to work full-time. I, Susan, ran into the editor one day on the street. The time had run out on her maternity leave. "I've resigned," she said, beaming, as if an enormous burden had simply vanished. Not long afterward, I had a very different encounter with the executive. She was headed back to work after a three-month leave. Her three-month-old was in the hands of an able in-home sitter. Her two older boys—three and five—were piled in the car, headed for day care. She wasn't happy. Although I don't recall her exact words, she was, she said, not ready.

These were, we thought, troubling signs. Obviously, the management-level women at our office do not constitute a scientific sample. Nor do the new mothers we happen to know make a trend. But in combination they suggested something we knew all too well: our society hasn't figured out how to make life easier for working parents.

At that time, we were very optimistic about our own job arrangement. It seemed to solve everybody's problems. By splitting a five-day week we had managed to create time for our families. Our employers, who had been trying to fill this full-time post for six months, now had not one but two experienced people for the price of one. We were also encouraged by recent news reports. IBM had just introduced a three-year extended-leave benefit. Employees had the option of working part-time for up to three years for family-related or other reasons. Du Pont released dramatic results from a corporate survey indicating that both men and women wanted more flexibility. The company, a leader in what have been dubbed "family-friendly" policies, was prepared to give them more options. Good news, we thought.

Around the same time, Felice Schwartz, president of Catalyst, Inc., a research and advisory service, opened Pandora's box with an article in the *Harvard Business Review* entitled "Management Women and the New Facts of Life." Speaking primarily to the corporate community, she called for "family supports," including realistic maternity leaves, paternity leaves, flexibility, relocation assistance for two-career couples, flexible benefits, and what she called "the primary ingredient," child care. All of which seemed quite reasonable to us.

But she also called for the establishment of separate career paths for "career primary women" and family-oriented women. One would be a fast track; the other would be a more flexible track, a slow track, or, as the *New York Times* called it, a "Mommy Track." Not surprisingly, feminists were outraged. Such a track could set women back two decades to an era when they were doomed to second-class jobs and second-rate pay scales. What would happen to the women who wanted none of this Mommy Track business? And, would women with families automatically be viewed as slow-track material? If, as Schwartz argued, career-primary women were to be identified early in their careers, how were corporations to make such distinctions? The media picked up on the controversy and for a time elevated the Mommy Track to superstardom. From *Nightline* on down to *Donahue*, everybody was talking about it. The Mommy Track debate raised a lot of important issues, some simple, some complex. The questions that most provoked us were these very basic ones:

❑ Is it possible for most women to have a successful career and raise a family?

❑ How much is American business willing to bend to the needs of working families?

❑ If women opt for more flexibility, will we lose our bid for equality?

❑ If we maintain the status quo, will women ultimately end up going back home?

Not surprisingly, these are the same questions that came up when we did our not-so-scientific survey of our place of work and the new moms we know.

Betty Friedan, prescient as she is, raised most of these questions ten years ago in her book *The Second Stage*. Unless we find a way to integrate work and family and to pull men into a new feminist agenda, she argued, all may well be lost. Like Friedan, we're not ready to abandon the goals of economic, political, and social equality for women. But we can't help but wonder why doctrinaire feminists keep coming out on the wrong side of issues that affect working women. In the Mommy Track debate, Friedan's voice was, in our minds, the voice of reason. She was optimistic but not unrealistic when she told Ted Koppel: ". . . the cutting edge is not a 'mommy track,' which is really another word for sex discrimination. The cutting edge is more flexible work options offered to women—and men." This book is about whether such options exist today and, if not, how to make them happen.

IT'S NOT JUST A WOMEN'S ISSUE ANYMORE

In 1980, when my first child was two, I, Susan, was working as an editor at *Memphis* magazine. Every month it fell upon me to come up with a feature story. Like most working mothers with toddlers, I was preoccupied with the subject of child care. It had taken me months to find someone I trusted to take care of my newborn son. I had interviewed no fewer than fifty people for an in-home sitter job. When he was eighteen months old, I began the quest for day care. That was even more difficult. The waiting lists were long at the best centers and the wait could run as much as a year. There were no day-care hot lines or referral services. Little significant help existed in weeding out the good centers from the bad. Getting a day-care license, I found, had more to do with zoning, fire codes, and minimal staff–child ratios than any measure of the quality of care. I had gone through young adulthood assuming that, once I was ready for child care, child care would be there for me. I was stunned.

At that time, there were only 1.6 million spaces in U.S. day-care centers and more than 7 million small children with working mothers. This was, I thought, an important issue that merited coverage in a feature story. The rest of the staff thought otherwise. Controversy was hardly the problem. Winner of a national magazine award for a story on race relations, *Memphis* magazine was more than willing to tackle controversial subjects. We had already run stories on the abortion debate, the rise of the Christian right, and the pressures on interracial couples. Nor was it too mundane. *Memphis* was not above publishing a story on recycling or how to buy a used car.

No, the problem was something else altogether. The rest of the staff thought it was a woman's subject. "This is not *Redbook* or *Good Housekeeping*," I was told at one staff meeting. It took me months to convince them that day care was a subject worthy of coverage. Only after the day-care crisis appeared on the cover of *Time* magazine did the executive editor ruefully agree to publish the story.

We have come a long way since 1980. Child care is no longer considered "just a women's issue." Not long ago, when we attended a national conference on work and family where corporate representatives comprised the largest segment in the audience, the subject of child care dominated the agenda. After all, child care is now a legitimate corporate concern. Businesses have determined that it behooves them to take steps to make sure their employees' children are taken care of, because it means less absenteeism, lower turnover, higher productivity.

Consider these numbers. In 1978, only 110 companies had child-care policies or programs such as on-site centers, referral programs, community child-care support, or pretax payment programs. In 1990, little more than a decade later, 5,400 companies reportedly offer some form of child-care assistance, up from 2,500 in 1986. We're not just talking about major corporations; a recent survey by the American Society of Personnel Administrators (ASPA), which represents small and medium-sized firms, found that 50 percent of those surveyed were planning some kind of child-care-related program.

While the child-care problem has hardly been resolved, it has become an acceptable subject in business circles, spawning all kinds of activities. Here are a few examples of the hundreds of programs that have emerged over the past decade.

❏ The California Child Care Initiative, a public-private partnership involving thirty-three organizations, has put more than $3 million into a program to fund resource and referral agencies. As a result, 7,900 new child-care spaces have been created throughout the state.

❏ In 1990, B.E.&K., Inc., a construction company based in Birmingham, Alabama, set up a temporary child-care center fashioned out of a series of trailers at a construction site in Georgia. Eleven percent of the workers at the Port Wentworth center were women, and finding child care that suits a construction worker's hours is no easy task, so B.E.&K. came up with this novel solution.

❏ Six New York firms—including Colgate-Palmolive, Time Inc. Magazines, Ernst & Young, and the law firm of Skadden Arps Slate Meagher & Flom—have banded together to offer an emergency child-care service to more than 13,000 employees in New York and New Jersey.

❏ At Hewitt Associates, a nationwide human resources consulting firm, there's a full-time parent consultant on the staff to help with issues like child care, and if an associate has to hire a sitter in order to work late or take an overnight trip, the company pays the cost of the child care.

Reminds one executive: "A company may tell the press they're doing this because they care about their people, but there's always a business reason." In the case of child care, studies have linked inadequate child care with everything from absenteeism to on-the-job stress. One Gallup poll, commissioned in 1986 by *Fortune* magazine, found that more than half (52 percent) of all absenteeism among two-income couples with children under twelve was for family-related reasons. And two-income couples with children under twelve make up a growing proportion of the labor force. Individual companies have discovered that the cost of ignoring the child-care problem can be high. According to a study by The Los Angeles Department of Water and Power, the agency paid out $1 million in one year to people who were absent because of child care.

Child care is fast becoming a men's issue, a family issue, even a pressing social issue. But the next frontier is flexibility. Indeed, business interest in day care marks the beginning of a willingness to deal with a broad range of family-related matters. "Until very recently," says Ellen Galinsky, copresident of the Families and Work Institute, "most jobs were made more flexible for work-related reasons. But companies are just beginning to grapple with flexibility and to see the work/family connection. First they dealt with the issue of child care. I think the new horizon is flexibility."

There's evidence as well that this is an issue that concerns both sexes.

❏ In the 1986 *Fortune* survey of dual-income families with children under twelve, 30 percent of the men and 26 percent of the women had refused a promotion, transfer, or new job because it would have meant less time with their families.

❏ A nationwide 1989 *Washington Post*/ABC News poll found that more than half (56 percent) of the working mothers surveyed and *43 percent of the working fathers* had cut back on their hours in order to be with their children.

❑ Most striking—and highly publicized—were the findings of Robert Half International, recruiters in the field of finance, accounting, data processing, and banking. They found that nearly eight of ten American men and women would be willing to sacrifice "rapid career growth" to spend more time with their families. In fact, nearly 75 percent of the men opted for a slower career path where they could set their own *full-time* hours and spend more time with their families. All of which suggests that the Mommy Track should have been dubbed the Parent Track.

The message is simple: *I need more time. Time at home. Time for me. But, more than anything else, time with my children.* Most of the people we spoke with who had switched to more flexible careers had not been unhappy with their work or with their lives. What they seemed to want, more than anything else, was more control over how their children were being raised. Time with the kids: That's a luxury to today's two-income couples.

JOB FLEXIBILITY: *A PRESSING SOCIAL ISSUE*

Flexibility is not an issue that affects only a handful of people. Nearly 40 percent of the labor force now consists of two-income households where nobody's home to meet the repair man, pick up the dry cleaning, or cook the dinner. In fact, fewer than 7 percent of American families fall into the traditional pattern where the father goes to work, the mom stays home with the kids, cookies get baked, and dinner becomes a sit-down affair. The days of Ozzie and Harriet, of June Cleaver and the happy tribe on *Father Knows Best*, are gone. Wishing them back is not going to solve anyone's problem.

And yet, the world is still not designed for working parents. Despite twenty-four-hour supermarkets and Sunday hours at the mall, we still operate as if everyone had a wife at home to take care of the children. Routine visits to the doctor and dentist are not weekend excursions; they require time off from work. Schools typically close at 2:30 or 3 P.M.; offices usually shut down later. Given that fact, as well as the need for summer day care and sick care, fully 33 percent of the children of working parents have more than one child-care arrangement. But that in itself is not the problem.

Sometimes it seems as if life is made needlessly complex. Take my hometown of Washington, D.C., which has the highest percentage of two-income families in the United States. In Washington, most schools open at 9 A.M. Most offices open at 8:30. In other words, things are backward. The kids have to be at school thirty minutes after their parents arrive at work. As a result, many area parents are forced to make *before*-school child-care arrangements as well as *after*-school arrangements. Were the two starting times simply reversed, it would save working parents needless headaches and introduce a greater sense of continuity into the lives of their children.

Our jobs, too, are still designed around old patterns. The hours we work, and more important, where we do our work haven't changed significantly in twenty years, despite the mass entry of women into the labor force. That's partly because the upper ranks of management are still dominated by married men with wives at home, a subject we'll explore in Chapter 3. It's also because, even as feminism has opened doors for women, the desire for equality has made it difficult for women to ask for concessions from their employers. To admit things weren't working was to admit defeat. After all, how can you succeed at work if you bring your family problems to the office?

Many parents imagined they were alone. Says Ellen Galinsky of the Families and Work Institute: "In the early eighties I interviewed a lot of parents and began to see [conflicts between work and family] as a silent and powerful issue for American families. Mostly they felt that they ought to bear the brunt of it, that it was their own lack of confidence that was causing the problem, and that it was a personal issue, not a social issue."

But something's clearly awry if our working hours and workstyles operate against the best interests of *most* families. Already, two-thirds of all mothers work and more than half of the mothers with children under six now work, up from 30 percent in 1970. This is not a personal problem anymore.

More important, women make up a growing segment of

the labor force. Since 1980, women have taken 80 percent of the new jobs created in the economy. That pattern is expected to hold through the 1990s. If it does, women will make up the majority of the U.S. labor force by the year 2000. This, then, is a major social issue.

2

THE CHANGING NEEDS OF A CHANGING WORK FORCE

REALITY VS. RHETORIC: THE FEMINIST QUESTION

Mary Billings went to an Ivy League college in the early seventies, the peak of the women's movement. Her feminist credentials are impeccable. Graduating in 1974 with an independent major in Women and Media, Billings's first job broke ground for women: she became the first female sports writer at a big-city paper.

Seven years later, she became the first reporter at another major midwestern daily to go part-time. She's no longer alone. In fact, much to her dismay, many of the most experienced women reporters now work part-time because they want more time at home. "It concerns me a lot, because it can send a bad message to management, that when you have a family you're going to cut back," says Billings. "It also sends a dangerous message to the younger women, that you can't work and have a family. I'm afraid a lot of them are just planning to quit when they have kids."

Billings made the switch in 1982, not long after her first child was born. "I went back to work after my maternity leave and started weaning my son. He immediately got sick. For the first three months that I worked full-time, he was in family day care. He got sicker and sicker. Finally, he got pneumonia and ended up in the hospital for two weeks," says Billings. By then, she was petitioning for a part-time job. A political writer, she took a step down into a part-time copy editing post. But that didn't last long. She worked her way through three other beats at the paper, including sharing a job as an investigative reporter with another working mother. She's now a part-time columnist with the business section. Is her career successful? Although she's moved around within the paper, changing part-time assignments as often as every two years, many of the moves have been lateral and, she comments, "I haven't made editor."

What happened to her aspirations? Mary Billings maintains that the problem lies in our institutions. "The women are working," says Billings. "But the support services aren't there. It's not just child care. I mean the basics—coming home at six o'clock and trying to start dinner and housecleaning. A lot of things are going to have to change to make life easier for the two-income couple."

Billings is not the only woman who has struggled with the issue of feminist politics versus the reality of life as a working mother. Like the authors, she is part of that first generation of modern feminists. Our hopes, attitudes, and expectations have been mirrored in the media and defined by series of pat catch phrases. We've lived through the Superwomen myth. We alternately accepted and abandoned the concept of "quality time." Some of us watched as our biological time clocks ticked away. We suffered, we were told, from the Cinderella Complex and fear of success. We've been warned that if we didn't get married soon, all the men would be gone. Now we're working the second shift, and the word is out that we can't have it all, as if having it all were some kind of sin. We are the pioneers of the modern women's movement, the test cases, the people who, with or without families, had to find out for ourselves what works and what doesn't.

Unfortunately, a lot of women have found that working full-time, nonstop, and having a family doesn't work. In researching this book, we encountered a fair amount of disappointment, particularly among women in their late thirties and early forties whose ideals were shaped during the early seventies. "Feminism failed to teach us how to make choices," said one. "We were sold a bill of goods on day care," said another. "This Superwoman business is baloney," said a third.

DEFINING THE PROBLEM

The truth is, for working mothers life hasn't always been easy. That's not to say that all working women are unhappy or that it's impossible to juggle a successful career and a happy home life.

SOME WOMEN *DO* "HAVE IT ALL"

A 1989 Yankelovich poll conducted for *Time*/CNN revealed that 43 percent of the 1,000 women polled would describe themselves as "having it all"—marriage, children, and a successful career. Among those who didn't have it all yet, 45 percent at least expected to have it all someday.

But having it all depends on myriad factors. Countless books have been written about the crisis of working mothers and the struggle to balance home and work. From these, we can only conclude that Superwoman *does* exist. Given the obstacles, the fact that women have achieved so much in the past two decades is a testament to their dedication, ingenuity, and talents.

Here are just a few examples of the stumbling blocks working mothers have faced in their bid for equality.

Housework. Mundane as it may be, housework is no small issue and women still do most of it. As has now been confirmed by exhaustive research, working mothers have no *time.* For her book *The Second Shift,* Arlie Hochschild added the time it takes to do a paid full-time job, housework, and child care, averaging estimates from major time studies done in the sixties and seventies. She discovered that women worked roughly fifteen hours longer each week than men. Over a year, they worked *an extra month of twenty-four-hour days.* Unfortunately, the presence of a husband seemed to add to, not reduce, the burden.

Guilt. While the Ozzie and Harriet models may be approaching extinction, their image lives on in the consciousness of the typical American mother. Stress, guilt, anxiety, and conflicts, we are told in book after book, haunt the working mother. Whether they work or stay at home, American women take the job of mothering very seriously. *The Motherhood Report,* a nationwide study of more than 1,000 mothers, reveals that, contrary to popular belief, mothers who stay home are relatively unconflicted about being full-time moms; 70 percent reported no conflicts about being home full-time. Working mothers, on the other hand, were split almost fifty-fifty, with the majority swinging toward the side of conflict. Fully 55 percent "experienced moderate to very strong conflict about the fact that they had to leave their children every day to go to work."

STRESS AND THE WORKING WOMAN

According to a report released in February 1988 by the Bureau of National Affairs, the number one health risk for working women is stress, and the major cause of that stress is the act of balancing work and home.

About Men. What about men? Where do they fit into the picture? What happened to that new American man, that sensitive soul who was willing to help raise the kids, clean the house, and cook the dinner? Did he disappear into the Me Decade? Unfortunately, most studies support that view.

One, conducted by Dianne Burden and Bradley Googins of Boston University in 1987, found that married men *who live in the same house with their children* don't spend any more time with their kids than a father who is *not* living with his children. They also found that husbands of working women spend no more time with their children than do the husbands of homemakers. They don't spend more time helping around the house either. Says The Boston University Job and Homelife Study: "No significant difference was found between married males with employed wives and those with nonemployed wives on hours per week the husband spends on home chores (about 12 hours for both groups)."

Johanna Freedman raises the question "Where's Daddy?" in *The Parental Leave Crisis,* and answers with a depressing litany of studies and the conclusions they present:

❑ In two-parent families in which the mother is at home, the father spends only 20 percent to 25 percent as much time with his children as does his wife.

❑ Many studies show that fathers assume essentially no responsibility for child care.

❑ Even when both parents are employed thirty or more hours per week, the amount of responsibility assumed by fathers appears to be "as negligible" as when mothers are unemployed.

Anecdotal evidence suggests that men are beginning to share more responsibility for the children, the home, and the transportation. In fact, as corporations begin to explore these issues, they're finding that men are starting to register stress over the balancing act.

We suspect that, while men are helping, they're just not helping enough. It may have more to do with underestimating the magnitude of the job—picking up the kids, taking them to buy shoes, food shopping, cooking, cleaning, bedtime stories, baths, doctors, dentists, health, and happiness—than a deliberate shirking of responsibilities. Then there's this issue of guilt again. We suspect that some working mothers are not willing to give up, say, the bedtime ritual with their children *when they haven't seen those children all day.*

Child Care. The prevailing attitude among the women we interviewed was this: no matter how good your child-care arrangement, it's not Mom. That's a rather strong cultural, perhaps also maternal, bias against working mothers. We also encountered a lot of this: "I'd go crazy if I were home every day, but I'd go crazy if I had to work eight hours every day. I'd never see my kids." No one told us they cut back work because of a child-care problem. They told us instead that they wanted to be more involved in raising their children. But scratch the surface, press a little, and the child-care woes come pouring out.

What I, Susan, didn't know back in 1980, when I was preoccupied with my personal child-care crisis, was that the search for child care goes on and on and on. When I first interviewed Mary Billings, I thought her case was extreme. She's had fifteen child-care arrangements for her two children in seven years. But then I added up the child-care arrangements my son has had during his first eleven years. He's had nine—and I have only worked a traditional forty-hour week for three of those eleven years.

Finding child care is the first problem; keeping it, the second. Consistency, the foundation of any secure child-care arrangement, is a problem. Turnover rates for day-care workers average 40 percent. Turnover among in-home caregivers is not much better. Carollee Howes, a psychologist at UCLA, found that, among children eighteen to twenty-four months old cared for in their own homes or family day-care homes, most had already experienced two to three changes in caregivers. Some had already had as many as six.

Child care can be unreliable. *Fortune* magazine's 1986 child-care study found that 40 percent of the parents surveyed had experienced a breakdown in their child-care arrangement in the previous three months. That's no small issue from the perspective of employer or employee. Absenteeism is one obvious result. Stress is another. *New York Times* columnist Anna Quindlen eloquently describes the relationship between a mother and her child-care arrangement: "Competent care of their children is the superstructure upon which working mothers build every bit of the rest of their lives," she writes. "We say, 'The day-care center is closing,' when the sentence really means 'The underpinnings of my life are gone.' " Unfortunately, as too many working mothers know all too well, the child-care superstructure is very weak.

Quality is a problem. For example, in 1985, when the Du Pont Company surveyed its Delaware-based employees on their child-care needs, the company found 28 percent of parents dissatisfied with the educational quality of the care available. Researchers at Bank Street College found that 47 percent of the parents surveyed at three companies felt finding quality care was a "significant" or "major" problem.

Of course, day care is not the only option. Among working parents, only one-fifth use licensed day-care centers. Others rely on a mix of friends, relatives, neighbors, and paid sitters at home or at a neighbor's house. That is, at least in part, because of lack of space in quality centers. But it may also be a matter of choice.

Increasingly, parents seem to be concerned about the consequences of early day-care experiences. Some of the mothers we interviewed had strong reservations about having their children in day care full-time. Said Nadine Davis, an assignment

---

HOW DO PARENTS FEEL ABOUT DAY CARE?

A 1989 nationwide *Washington Post*/ABC News poll found that, among parents with children under fourteen, about one-third (39 percent) felt day care had negative consequences; another third (36 percent) felt it had no effect; and only one-fifth (22 percent) saw some benefits to the child. Among parents with preschool-aged children, just under a third felt day care has positive effects.

editor who works two days a week at an East Coast television station: "I think the media have been unfair regarding the effects of group care on children. A preponderance of evidence says that if you put a bunch of kids together of different ages with relatively little supervision, you get kids who are aggressive and have serious problems in the trusting category."

The debate surrounding the effects of day care has escalated in recent years. Gone are the days when working parents could naively assume that day care was good, because it fostered independence and early socialization. That, at least, was what the early day-care reports told us. Now, the first generation has passed through the system, and they are being scrutinized by the experts. The news is not good. Recent studies have linked a day-care upbringing with aggressiveness, poor peer relations, discipline problems, poor work habits, and antisocial behavior, particularly in boys.

Once the hope of an entire generation of feminists, day care has, in some circles at least, become a dirty word. "Can you imagine," a thirty-four-year-old executive recently asked me with a note of utter disgust, "having to put your child in one of those awful day-care centers?" Said another, a forty-year-old feminist with two day-care-reared sons: "It's funny. Whenever I talk about my sons' day-care center, I always add a qualifier. I hear myself saying, as if I'm apologizing, 'But it's a really good day-care center.' "

What about help in the home? The myth of the high-powered two-career couple with a full-time, in-home, forever faithful nanny is just that. Only 6 percent of families have full-time help to care for the kids. Then there's the issue of supervision. As one part-timer told us: "At-home child care is the only unsupervised position in the world. If you're looking for a substitute for yourself, forget it."

Good, reasonably priced, stable child care and child-care referral is an essential element of any culture that claims to support the working family. *Almost 70 percent of American children now have two working parents. It's difficult to avoid the obvious question: Who is going to take care of these children?*

Latchkey Kids. Many working parents thought they'd have things licked when the kids went off to school. But, as numerous part-timers told us, that was when things really began to snap. Ours is a car-pool culture, and getting the kids from school to Scouts, sports, or ballet can strain even the most ingenious parent. Again, support services are a problem. Perhaps for economic reasons, including the high cost of insurance, transportation services for children have not materialized. Some working parents rely on taxicabs. Others rely on other parents. In many cases, it's up to the child to get from one place to another.

Nicole Payne, who until recently managed the Alternative Work Options program for the state of Massachusetts, claims the latchkey crunch hasn't even hit yet. "Right now we're seeing a lot of thirty-five-year-old women having their first babies [looking for part-time options]. They thought they would just keep right on as if nothing had happened, but suddenly there's a full-time job at home too. We're going to have another eye opener when all these infants and toddlers get into school. Their parents think that's the end. But that's the beginning. We see six-year-olds walking home from school by themselves and staying alone. That's a problem and someone's going to have to deal with it."

THE LATCHKEY CRISIS

According to U.S. Census data, 1 million American children are unsupervised while their parents are at work. Among the children of working parents, *43 percent of those aged six to twelve* and *76 percent of teenagers* apparently lack any adult supervision after school, according to one study.

Given the numbers regarding quality child care and latch-key kids, it's not surprising that many parents are concerned about their children while they're at work. Boston University researchers found about one-quarter of the working parents they studied "are worrying about their children while they are at work either *always or most of the time*." Obviously, that stress is going to have some impact on productivity. It's also going to have some impact on the people involved.

Flexibility can't solve all these problems. But it seems to help. It can mean any number of alternative arrangements.

The 80-Percent Solution. Some families find relief when one parent cuts back to a four-day week. Says Jane Rosenthal, who works four days a week as a conservator at a major federally funded museum: "One Saturday I was stuck in traffic and I said to myself, 'This is nuts!' I was running errands along with every other working mother in town." So now she's off every Friday. "I go to the supermarket, get the household in order, take care of dentist appointments and doctor visits. Then I have the weekends for the family and I don't take time off from work for personal business."

The 50-Percent Solution. For other parents, particularly those with children in school full-time, a workday that ends at 2:30 can eliminate the need for child care altogether. Marian Brescia has had such an arrangement with the Montgomery County, Maryland, government for nineteen years, where she's moved up from a secretarial to a professional level, earning $31 an hour. "I guess I did it before it was fashionable. Back then, we were supposed to be like men. The only problem was, I wanted to be home when my kids got home from school," she says.

Like Brescia, I had a 9:30 to 2:30 workday for several years, filling in from home when deadlines demanded it. Why? My eight-year-old son's day was turning into a fifteen-hour marathon—school, after-school program, sports, and homework, which was becoming a late-night event. My part-time schedule freed up his afternoons.

The 99.9-Percent Solution. For parents on the fast track, a forty-hour work week feels like a part-time job. Not long ago, I clipped a newspaper story regarding round-the-clock day-care programs—night care, if you will. A lawyer, a woman with a three-year-old daughter, was quoted regarding the pressing need for after-day-care day-care programs. Often, she said, she found it difficult to leave the office before nine or ten at night. Her husband, also an attorney, had the same problem. It's not unusual for a lawyer to work such hours and not surprising that many of the first Mommy Track slots were created in law firms.

Says Nancy Wolf, another Washington attorney, who scaled back to a forty-hour week with every other Friday afternoon off ("when it's feasible"): "I think the whole problem is Federal Express. There was a time when the last Federal Express left around five P.M. Then they upped the deadline to seven P.M. A couple of years later they changed it to nine P.M., so everybody stayed in the office until nine. Now, you can give a package to Purolator until one in the morning. The irony is, half the time, no one really needs it for two weeks. We're being assaulted by our own ability to communicate." In such an environment, a high-powered job can mean a commitment of sixty, seventy, or eighty hours a week. For many working parents, such a schedule holds little appeal. Some are more than willing to trade off income and advancement potential for an eight-hour workday. But just how high a price should they have to pay to work near-normal hours? That's a question we'll explore in Part II.

The 100-Percent Solution. From an employer's perspective, job-sharing and telecommuting can be the best flexible solutions. With job-sharing, the people are part-time but the job itself remains full-time. Telecommuting, or working from home via technology, can mean any number of combinations of in-office and work-from-home options, including full-time arrangements. But, like job-sharing, telecommuting remains relatively rare, despite futurist predictions of in-home offices equipped with fax machines, computers, and modems for home–office communication.

Of course, not all flexible options are new. Experiments in job-sharing date back to the early 1970s and flextime has been institutionalized in quite a few American offices. In 1988, almost 12 percent of all workers were on flextime. Researchers have found that flextime, where employees have the option of coming in early or late while working a standard eight-hour day, offers little in the way of *actual* relief for working parents. That is primarily because of the rigidity of the child-care system, according to Graham Staines, who did much of the ground-breaking research on flextime. Asks Staines rhetorically: "What good is flexible work if the rest of life is inflexible?"

Certainly, the concept of part-time work, too, is nothing new. Anyone who works in an office knows that part-time clerical and administrative jobs have served as a veritable ghetto for generations of women. In 1977, women working full-time earned a median wage of $3.92 an hour; for women working part-time, that figure was $3.09. Now labeled the "contingent labor force," the ranks of temporary and low-paying part-time jobholders have swelled in recent years as business attempts to respond to short-term economic contractions and expansions. These jobs are, by their very nature, second-class, offering little in the way of job security and, generally, nothing in the way of benefits.

But we're talking about something else altogether, a new part-time alternative, one that offers competitive salaries, benefits, and, in a surprising number of cases, the chance for career

---

WHAT DO WE MEAN BY FLEXIBILITY?

- ❑ Flextime
- ❑ Staggered hours
- ❑ Flexible hours
- ❑ Shortened work weeks
- ❑ Extended work weeks
- ❑ Compressed work weeks
- ❑ Part-time hours
- ❑ Job-sharing
- ❑ Telecommuting, or work from home

A glossary of these terms appears in Part III.

growth. These flexible arrangements are indisputably on the rise. Unfortunately, language is itself one of the barriers to rethinking these new arrangements. Tell someone you work "part-time" and they will assume you have no significant responsibilities and that you're off the career track altogether. Ironically, in many cases this alternative career path is open *only* to top performers and valuable employees—more a symbol of achievement than apathy.

If business is going to accommodate the people who need more flexibility, then we have to question some assumptions about how we work, where we work, and when we work. The questions are these:

❏ How can we fashion more equitable pay and benefit schedules for people who aren't willing to work ten hours a day, or even eight hours a day?

❏ How can we change the way we evaluate work so that it has more to do with what we produce and less to do with hours spent in the office?

❏ How can we change attitudes so that valuable part-time people are perceived as being just as valuable as full-time people?

❏ Is it possible to hop off the fast track and get back on later?

❏ And, finally, how can we change attitudes so that the measure of a man, as well as of a woman, is not inextricably tied to *time spent on the job?*

The good news is this: some employers are already beginning to ask and find answers to these questions.

THE BOTTOM LINE: THE BUSINESS
REASONS FOR FLEXIBLE JOBS

Ask anyone who wants to scale back and you'll find it has very little to do with what's happening at work. Most parents don't perceive flexibility as a business issue. They see it as a personal problem, a family issue. Why should business accommodate their needs? The business reasons, in corporatese, are these:

❑ To recruit and retain talented people

❑ To reduce turnover and absenteeism

❑ To increase productivity

The key word here is *retain*. Business is losing employees to its own inflexibility.

Cathy Crawford, the Experienced Recruiting Programs Manager in Human Resource Staffing you met earlier, is a typical example. Before going part-time, she petitioned her boss at the division level for a shorter work week. The answer was no. "I was prepared to quit," she says. "Now I know I really would have had to. I have a one-hour commute, so it turns into a ten- or eleven-hour day. My kids sleep twelve hours a day, so basically, that would have meant they wouldn't see me all week long." Instead of leaving, Crawford took a part-time opening in another part of the company. She, in fact, replaced a full-time manager who *did* resign a month after returning from maternity leave. While not technically a job-share, Crawford's position was split into two jobs, both now held by working mothers who wanted to work less.

Karen Nappi was less fortunate. A publications manager for an East Coast trade association, Nappi petitioned her boss for a shorter work week in 1981, following the birth of her first child. She's now a full-time mother. "I made a formal proposal to restructure my job," says Nappi. "Then I checked back every three weeks. That went on for five and a half months. What was their response? They offered me a promotion. I said, 'You don't understand. I want to work less.' I ended up leaving. I had an outstanding work record and I was a bit shocked that they would just blow me off. But that's what they did."

Where are these women going? Some, like Nappi, are throwing up their hands in dismay and heading home. Others, like Glenda Elkins, are going to competitors who offer more flexibility. But, historically, a lot of women have been entering the ranks of the self-employed. In the five years from 1977 to

1982 the number of women running their own businesses rose 39 percent to 2.9 million. Says Kathleen Christensen, who interviewed scores of women who work at home for her book *Women and Home-Based Work:* "What's driving many of these women to become self-employed is the rigidity of the job structures. The majority of these women weren't starting a business so they could be entrepreneurs. They did it because they had so few options. Nine times out of ten they wanted more flexibility—part-time, job-sharing, work at home, anything. They couldn't get it. As a result, many of these women were not equipped to start their own businesses. They weren't prepared to put in the hours necessary to really build a business. So they were caught between a rock and a hard place."

Nationwide numbers are not available, but studies suggest that women are jumping in and out of the job market like wildfire in response to their families' needs. Audrey Vanden-Heuvel, a Ph.D. candidate at the University of North Carolina, published her thesis on that subject in 1989. She looked at the

THE PHILADELPHIA STORY

"The employer who clings to the idea of business as usual, forty hours, five days a week, will struggle through the 1990s," says Gil Gordon, a consultant in the field of telecommuting, or work-from-home, who is helping the U.S. Air Force, the state of California, and the Washington State Energy Office set up pilot telecommuting programs. In 1989, Gordon did a proprietary study for a Philadelphia insurance company. "We talked to women who had left the company with good work records. We asked them whether they had discussed the possibility of work at home or telecommuting with their boss. Either they said no or the boss said no. We asked, If the company provided some kind of flexible arrangement—job-sharing, telecommuting, part-time hours—would they be interested in coming back on that basis? *Sixty percent* said they would consider returning."

home/work patterns of several thousand mothers during the seven-year period following the birth of their first child. She found that, at some point during those seven years, the vast majority of those mothers worked full-time. Among those same mothers, the vast majority also stayed home full-time during some of those years. Some worked early in their children's lives. Some worked later. Others alternated between working and staying home. But, instead of a consistent pattern of home/work combinations, she found an astonishing number of variations. She broke down her analysis by race and number of children. Among white women with one child, as an example, she found more than 600 different home/work patterns, all variations in the timing of these moves in and out of the labor force. The challenge for employers is to come up with some alternatives that will keep more women employed long-term and enable them to follow a more consistent career path.

Certainly, losing a few good women would mean little if American business had plenty of trained, talented people. But that's no longer the case. We're facing an acute labor shortage. When the American Society of Personnel Administrators conducted a survey of its members in 1988, they found that more than half were having trouble filling their job openings. Nearly half of the companies surveyed (44 percent) reported difficulty finding executives and managers; more than half were having trouble finding professionals, and a dramatic 66 percent were having problems finding technical and technical-support people.

But the worst is yet to come. By the year 2000, population growth and the expansion of the labor force will hit their lowest point in fifty years. According to *Workforce 2000,* published by the Hudson Institute, during this decade the labor force will grow by only 1 percent per year, as compared with 2.9 percent per year in the high-growth seventies.

In this decade, the last of the baby boomers will come of age and the baby bust will hit. Shortages will be most severe among the highly educated. From 1985 to the mid-nineties, the number of college graduates is expected to decline 8 percent, while economic growth in the 25 percent range is predicted. The demand for professional, technical, and sales jobs will increase, putting more pressure on American business.

And, just as important, the character of the labor market will change. By the end of this decade, only 15 percent of the U.S. labor force will consist of American-born white males. The vast majority of new entrants in the labor force will be women and minorities. Unless things change, the pressure to find solutions to the work-vs.-family dilemma will be enormous.

3

FROM THE INSIDE OUT: RESHAPING THE WORKPLACE

THE NEW FACTS OF CORPORATE LIFE

In 1970, when I, Susan, was preparing to go off to college, I spent a summer weekend with my parents and several houseguests. One of them, I'll call him Jim Smith, was the president of a major multinational corporation, and as smart, savvy, and conservative a fellow as one might imagine in such a post. One evening, after a little wine and a hearty meal, the conversation turned to the budding feminist movement and what lay ahead. I waxed rhetorical.

Jim Smith, wise to the ways of corporate America, focused on the practical. Equality won't work, he maintained. Ultimately, his argument boiled down to a single question, What will happen when one half of a couple—man or woman—is transferred by a corporation? You have to move to move up, he argued. What will happen to the husband or wife? Will he or she simply up and leave an equally substantial job? Will they refuse the move and derail one career in the interests of the other? What if a corporate climber is married to a professional, a doctor or lawyer, say? Will the professional willingly give up a thriving practice and follow?

It was an issue that had never occurred to me and certainly not one on which I was willing to hang the future of feminism. I was stumped. Well, I arched my back defensively and declared, "They'll refuse the transfer." Then I thought of something else: they could live in different cities temporarily. Finally, I hit upon an argument that satisfied me: corporations will have to change. They won't be able to move people like pawns on a chessboard anymore. Given that Mr. Smith had undoubtedly moved a dozen times in his professional life, taking wife and children along, he responded as if this particular answer bordered on the absurd.

But, of course, corporations can and do change. For one thing, it's not called a transfer anymore. It's called *relocation*. And relocation surveys combined with a rise in refusals to relocate were early tip offs that a new generation had arrived on the corporate scene. As an example, about 40 percent of Mobil Oil Corporation's employees refused to move from New York to Virginia when the company changed its headquarters location. As part of a relocation and career-development study, Mobil found that 27 percent of men and 19 percent of women refused to relocate at the company's request.

"The normal way of conducting business has been that someone calls you on Wednesday and says they want you to go to Timbuktu on Monday morning and you leave Friday," says Derek Harvey, manager of human resources at Mobil. "The traditional attitude has been: if you're offered the chance to relocate, you should take it." But, according to Harvey, that's not how two-income couples operate. "If I'm thirty-three and earning sixty thousand dollars a year, and I'm married to someone who's earning fifty to sixty thousand a year," he explains, "I don't want someone telling me that. Instead, I'd be apt to say, 'I'll consider it. I'll look at what's best for my spouse and myself and I'll let you know.' That's a very different attitude."

Mobil is not alone. Ask any executive if they're having more trouble with transfers than they were ten or fifteen years ago, and they'll affirm the trend. Proprietary research at Work/Family Directions, a Massachusetts-based consulting firm whose clients tend to fall in the Fortune 500 category, found that as many as 40 percent of corporate women with young children are unwilling to relocate.

What Jim Smith couldn't have guessed was how far some corporations would go to accommodate working couples. It was one thing when women were the only ones bucking the system. But, in increasing numbers, men are also resisting relocation. "It really came into focus when men started to be the trailing spouse," says Arlene Johnson of the Conference Board's Work and Family Center. "Then companies began to say, Yes, well, that really does hurt a person's career."

Attitudes and policies are beginning to change. For example, in 1989, when Jean Campbell's husband took a job in St. Louis, she didn't have to give up her job at Hewitt Associates, a Chicago-based consulting firm. The company found space for her at its St. Louis regional office. She kept her original job, as

---

CORPORATE RELOCATION: THE US SPRINT APPROACH

In 1989, US Sprint, which relocates about 900 people each year—5 percent of its total work force—announced one of the most progressive relocation policies in American industry. Aside from job counseling and placement services, the company would provide as much as $2,000 a month for up to two months to the displaced half of a couple, a category that includes not just spouses, but live-in heterosexual and homosexual partners as well. Obviously, few companies have gone to such lengths and many companies haven't changed at all. But more and more corporations are being forced to adapt to the new reality of the two-income couple with relocation programs.

a public relations specialist, traveling back to headquarters every week or two and communicating with the staff and field offices by phone or electronic mail. It's an arrangement subject to periodic review but one that could go on indefinitely. Again, when an executive at Mobil was transferred shortly before his baby's birth, the company put a hold on the move, setting up a computer terminal at his home and letting him work from there until after the blessed event. "We would never have considered something like that, even three years ago," says Mobil's Harvey.

THE NEW WORK/ FAMILY AGENDA

The relocation issue was one signal to American business that people's needs, values, and attitudes about work were changing. Most companies that are beginning to look at issues like child care, flexibility, and parental leave policies will tell you that they saw the need coming, that they were being "proactive" as opposed to reactive, and that the dawn of "Workforce 2000," the age when women and minorities will dominate the labor force, is already upon us. But, in fact, a number of companies have been propelled into change by a new set of realities. In other words, demographics forced the issue.

At some companies, a predominance of women pushed these issues onto the corporate agenda. Aetna Life & Casualty, which began developing progressive coping strategies in 1987, is 70 percent female and headquartered in the Northeast, where competition for the best people is particularly intense. Says Sherry Herchenroether, manager of family services at Aetna: "We were already feeling the pinch as far as the number of people who were applying for jobs and the quality we were seeing."

Others have had to rethink their parental leave strategies, precisely because they've been confronted with their own corporate baby booms. At Marriott Corporation, which launched a major study of parental leave policies in 1990, the company has projected 1,200 to 1,500 births among its 5,000 headquarters employees over the next five years. At Levi Strauss & Co., more than two-thirds of the company's merchandisers are women in their child-bearing years. Merchandising is a job that involves long hours and lots of travel, so Levi Strauss has launched a series of pilot programs in job-sharing and part-time alternatives for these employees.

More than a few corporations told us they examined their affirmative-action goals and found they were losing trained, promotable, talented women owing to a lack of flexible options. In the mid-eighties, Corning, Inc., found that women were leaving the company at twice the rate of men. "We didn't have alternate work arrangements, so if you couldn't work the standard forty- or eighty-hour week, if you wanted to work part-time, the answer was, 'No, we don't have part-time work,' " says Sherry Mosley, a human resources consultant at Corning. "So people were forced to make a decision—they could stay or leave. There wasn't any flexibility built into the system." In 1988, the company launched a program for salaried employees that incorporated reduced work schedules, among other things. Says Mosley: "Since we initiated the program, retention has

---

THE NEW WORK/ FAMILY BENEFITS

"Work/family," among those who make it their business to know, is the shorthand for a slew of programs and policies designed to help people balance home and work. They include:

❏ Parental leave policies

❏ Adoption assistance

❏ Eldercare programs

❏ Care for sick children

❏ Paid time off for family emergencies

❏ Relocation assistance

❏ Child care—subsidies, referral services, and on-site centers

❏ Flexibility and alternative scheduling

gone up. We've documented high-potential women who would probably have left the company and tried to get back in later."

Businesses are grappling with a rather complex set of issues:

- How to attract and keep top people from a shrinking labor pool.
- Why women and minorities are not moving up rapidly in their organizations and taking steps to change attitudes.
- How to reduce absenteeism and turnover and increase productivity at a time when an increasing number of employees are pulled between home and work.

To hear the consultants in the field of work/family tell it, business is booming. The Families and Work Institute, a non-profit research and consulting firm whose clients include Levi Strauss, Illinois Bell, Johnson & Johnson, and the state of New York, tells us corporations are knocking on their doors. Work/family is a hot topic. Reports Ellen Galinsky, copresident of the Families and Work Institute: "CEO attitudes are changing. I used to have fights at meetings about whether or not this was a legitimate business issue. Now I'm invited to speak to company executives, mostly men, about issues like the quality in early-childhood programs. It's no longer a question of whether they should or shouldn't get involved in work/family programs. It's becoming an issue that people are jockeying for power over,

---

ON-SITE CHILD CARE

As of 1990, thousands of companies, small and large, report-edly have on-site day-care facilities. Among major corpora-tions, Apple Computer, Campbell Soup, Stride Rite, Hoff-man-La Roche, and Johnson & Johnson are just a few of the firms that offer on-site day care. According to *Working Mother* magazine, SAS Institute, Inc., a North Carolina–based soft-ware product company, offers *free* on-site child care for chil-dren up to age five at its hundred-acre business campus.

which strikes me as funny." Funny because for so long, subjects like child care, how to care for sick children, spouse relocation, or job-sharing were taboo.

Taboo no more. The Families and Work Institute reports that 86 percent of 7,500 companies surveyed recently had plans to develop some kind of work/family program.

Of course, not everyone agrees that work/family stands at the top of the corporate agenda or at the top of employees' minds. "Most employees are still concerned about how the company treats them—basic issues like fair pay, competitive benefits, respect, and trust," says Dr. Eileen Gochman, vice-president and director of organization research at Opinion Research Corp., a consultant to major corporations. "Most companies don't even meet these basic needs yet. You don't expect a company that doesn't value your contribution and doesn't treat you fairly to start being concerned about your family."

In fact, when it comes to integrating flexibility into their *modus operandi*, hundreds of companies are doing something. Thousands are doing nothing. Only a handful, as Gochman contends, are doing everything right. In its 1988 survey of over

CHILD-CARE RESOURCE AND REFERRAL

When business began looking closely at the possibility of building and running on-site day-care centers, some companies were deterred by early research suggesting that people preferred day care near their homes over day care at work. Others were deterred by the high cost or the administrative nightmare of running a center. After all, not every business was willing to get into the day-care business. Resource and referral became the next best thing. Generally, businesses offer child-care resources and referral by contracting with local or nationwide consultants who in turn help employees locate day care, in-home sitters, or home-based child care in their communities. The service is generally free to employees.

500 member corporations, the Conference Board found only *four firms* that offered all six alternative work arrangements covered in the survey—part-time, flextime, compressed work week, phased retirement, job-sharing, and home-based work.

Not every company with a work/family agenda offers flexibility. We looked at more than 150 companies, many considered leaders in work/family. Some of these firms allow flexibility, but few encourage it. And some companies were downright discouraging. One prevailing attitude in such companies is this: if we take care of the child-care problem, the need for flexibility will go away. At American Bankers Insurance Group, whose on-site child-care center has earned them praise and publicity, flexible jobs are discouraged. "We offer such great benefits for child care, it's not necessary for them [parents] to work part-time," says Ellen Rifkin, a staffing coordinator at American Bankers. "They don't worry about child care because they have their children with them all day."

American Bankers' attitude points up another not uncommon approach: if we eliminate the sources of stress—child-care problems, sick-care problems, eldercare problems—we eliminate the need for flexibility. But that's really not the issue. Says the Conference Board's Arlene Johnson: "The goal is not for corporations to solve all our child-care and dependent-care needs so that we can keep longer and longer hours and work harder and harder, which I think is sometimes how the issue is perceived. You have to redefine the problem. The problem is that you've got a work force that has two responsibilities and always will. You can enable them to balance those two interests or everybody's the loser."

Flexibility is one of the best ways to assure some balance between these two worlds. So, it's not surprising that in the late eighties, as companies began tackling this whole issue of "work-vs.-family," the need for flexibility began bubbling up.

American Express began dealing with the child-care problem in 1984. They started off small, with low-risk, low-cost projects—like helping their people in New York City find child care by linking up with area resource and referral services. They followed that up with an employee survey on child care, building support for work/family issues. Finally, in 1989, they conducted a comprehensive, wide-ranging survey to find out more about what their employees needed. Says Rennie Roberts, senior vice-president of human resources for the corporation: "Flexibility was the clear, crying need that people expressed in our 1989 survey."

In 1987, Johnson & Johnson began to look at work/family issues for the first time. Heeding the lessons of some of the corporate pioneers and working closely with the Families and Work Institute, they surveyed their employees. Johnson & Johnson expected a need for child care to surface. But flexibility emerged as the top priority. Says Chris Kjeldsen, vice-president

---

SICK-CHILD CARE AT HONEYWELL

Very young children, according to Honeywell, Inc.'s Work and Family Guidebook, will get six to nine viral infections a year, lasting three to seven days each. That's somewhere between *eighteen and sixty-three sick days per year per child*. It's not surprising that leading-edge companies are devising policies that help working parents deal with the problem of sick children.

Such programs might mean contracting with a sitter service to provide in-home care, an alliance with a local hospital or sick-care center, an on-site sick-care facility, paid time off to care for sick children, or subsidizing the cost of sick care. Honeywell has made sick-child care a priority—in part because a high percentage of employees at Minneapolis headquarters are single parents. The company offers referrals to local sick-care facilities and an 80 percent subsidy to cover the cost—parents pay only $2.70 an hour of the $13.50-an-hour fee. In 1989, the sick-child care program cost Honeywell about $33,000. But, according to company calculations, the program saved over $88,000 in higher productivity and reduced absenteeism. Sick care is available for parents who feel they need to be at the office, but staying home is also an option.

of headquarters human resources at Johnson & Johnson: "The big issue that popped out was that of all the things that we would do as a corporation in support of parents, the biggest factor was that they wanted a flexible work schedule. I mean that's number one."

No company has amassed more data on its employees' work/family needs than the Du Pont Company. In 1985, senior management at Du Pont woke up to the child-care problem when a survey revealed that 70 percent of the company's employeees with children under thirteen used some form of child care *outside the home*. That number translates into one-fourth of the entire Du Pont work force. More than 60 percent of the Du Pont parents who use child care reported difficulty in finding care that fits their work schedules. The Delaware-based corporation responded with a number of programs, including the establishment of a statewide resource and referral agency for child care, which has since fielded 14,000 calls and become instrumental in expanding the number of child-care slots in Delaware.

With its 1988 employee survey, Du Pont became the first company to document a dramatic change in male attitudes and an intense interest in flexibility. "In 1988, we saw a rising concern among men about issues like who takes care of a sick child, arranging child care for overtime needs, coordinating people's vacations, travel relocation, everything," says Faith Wohl, director of the work-force partnering division of Du Pont employee relations. "We tapped into the major social transformation that is happening in this country, just by virtue of the two years in which we chose to survey."

Even among men, flexibility emerged as a major issue in 1988. *Fully 50 percent of the women and 25 percent of the men surveyed had considered leaving the company in search of more flexibility.* Employees expressed interest in more flexible parental leaves, professional part-time employment, flexible hours, and working from home. Among management-level women with children, more than half expressed an interest in part-time employment (with benefits) and more opportunities to work at home. "The need for flexibility," according to Wohl, "that was the most powerful message."

The Du Pont numbers tell us how quickly and drastically the work force is changing. But American industry is caught between two worlds, because, even today, Ozzie is found in disproportionate numbers in senior management.

We heard a lot of "Aha!" stories, like the one about the grandfather who began to understand the problem when his new granddaughter was put in a day-care center *fifty* hours a week, or about a father in senior management whose daughter was about to scrap her career aspirations because of work/family conflicts. We also heard a lot of human resources people bemoaning resistance from middle management and, until very recently, a lack of understanding from top management—one reason that surveys have played such a critical role in this process. Says one human resources manager: "Even within the human resources area, when you talk to some of the traditionalists in compensation and benefits about child care or eldercare or more flextime or part-time work, they look at you and say, 'You've got to be crazy. Why would we want to do that?'"

Indeed, the top slots in American business are still filled primarily by men—many with wives at home taking care of the kids. The higher up the corporate ladder someone sits, the less

---

CHILD-CARE INITIATIVES

Some major corporations set aside funds for community-based child-care initiatives; these might include training day-care providers, funding placement services, or equipping neighborhood centers. In 1989, IBM pledged $22 million to establish the IBM Child Care Resource and Development Fund to help increase the supply and improve the quality of child care in communities where the company has operations. AT&T's historic 1988 union contract, which called for a series of new work/family benefits, committed $5 million to funding local initiatives. Other corporate leaders with a commitment to supporting community child care include Du Pont, US West, and American Express.

PERSONAL TIME OFF

Time banks, personal time off, flexdays—call it what you will. At family-friendly companies, hourly employees can take time off for personal business or family emergencies and still get paid. US Sprint's new policy allows for a flexday, which can be taken in two- or three-hour increments for family emergencies. At Aetna Life & Casualty, personal time is left completely up to a supervisor's discretion.

---

likely he or she is to have to deal with work/family conflicts. Says the Boston University Job and Homelife Study: "The small minority of married men with wives at home are disproportionately represented in upper-management, high-salaried positions." And high percentages of women at the top are childless, single, or divorced.

CORPORATE POLICIES IN FLUX

Change in work/family programs is happening very fast. As we go to press in the fall of 1990, Levi Strauss, which already offers a lot of flexibility at its San Francisco headquarters, is undertaking its first major corporation-wide survey of employee needs. Honeywell has just announced the formation of a work/family task force. Apple Computer is only now creating a database in an effort to find out more about its flexible jobholders. Marriott has just begun a study of parental leave policies. Du Pont has established a task force on flexibility, dubbed the Flexteam. And Dow Chemical has just formed a management advisory counsel on women to address some of these issues. Corporate policies are in such a rapid state of change that, by the time this book is in print, more companies will undoubtedly have jumped on the flexibiity bandwagon.

It's not surprising, then, that corporate insiders who are pushing for change warn against optimism. Says Chris Kjeldsen, vice-president of human resources at Johnson & Johnson: "You're going to have to see the next generation move into the top [management] slots before you see a breakthrough."

THE THIRTY-SOMETHING GENERATION
AND THE QUEST FOR JOB FLEXIBILITY

Pushing up against the old school is a new generation. First to arrive on the corporate scene were these new-breed executives—motivated, educated women, the stepdaughters of radical feminism who donned business suits and polka-dot neckties in the seventies and worked their way up the ladder. Well into their thirties now, they led the push for flexibility. Says Laurie Margolies, corporate employee relations program manager at Digital Equipment: "They had the wisdom to know how the corporation works and the seniority to be in a position to understand the company and to mobilize their peers."

But it's the next generation—the under-thirty-five generation—that is forcing American companies to rewrite the rules governing everything from relocation to workplace flexibility. This is the postfeminist generation. Based on our discussions with the people who do the hiring for corporate America, this profile emerges.

❏ Despite their career aspirations, many young women are less willing to sacrifice family to career. "When I was growing up, everyone expected me to have a career. I was supposed to go to law school," one twenty-eight-year-old told us. Instead, she opted for full-time motherhood. "When it occurred to me that I could stay home, it was like a rush of freedom."

Companies have to work harder to attract these women and to keep them. First of all, they are less politically motivated; for many, feminism is not an issue. Second, their two-income status gives them the economic freedom to make choices. One human resources manager puts it this way: "A two-income couple who are thirty-five or under just seems to have a different way of operating and managing their lives. They're much more concerned about each other's careers *and* much more concerned about families. They're very rational in their decision-making."

❑ Ironically, it's the postfeminist women who have demanded—and won—some measure of equality on the home front. "We've seen a change in the last five or six years," says Sherry Herchenroether, who oversees the work/family program at Aetna Life & Casualty. "Couples are sharing responsibilities. They're both picking up and dropping off children. They're sharing in sick-child care. They're sharing in the decisions about what they're going to choose to do with their lives. And," adds Herchenroether, "I'm not sure the corporate world has understood that fully yet."

❑ Young men emerge as the new silent majority. When surveyed, their needs become clear: they too need relief from the stresses of working parenthood. But they're caught in a quandary. Scaling back hours, taking a paternity leave, or refusing to travel are hardly viewed as steps on the fast track. Despite all the talk about Daddy Tracks, out in the real world of business it is still not okay for a man to put his family ahead of his career. Reminds Barney Olmsted of New Ways to Work: "Culturally, it is much more acceptable for a woman to be on a flexible schedule and to work part-time in order to fulfill family responsibilities than it is for a man. A man's considered a wimp."

Young women have problems of their own. "Where does this fast track lead?" they ask themselves. And, "Is that where I want to be?" They look above them and see very few women in senior positions. Or, worse still, the committed female executives appear to be committed to one thing—their careers. Senior level women with families remain the rarity in American corporations. In fact, women have been more willing to make enormous sacrifices to promote their careers.

❑ One proprietary study at a major U.S. corporation showed that 65 percent of senior level women were childless; nearly half (43 percent) were unmarried.

❏ Another found that, while 94 percent of male managers in the forty-plus age group were married, only 57 percent of their female counterparts were married.

❏ At that same company, more than *90 percent* of women aged thirty-five to forty-five in management roles had no children.

"When I talk to the younger women, and I've been doing a lot of that lately, they say they are worried about doing it all," says a female senior executive who, for a time at least, successfully balanced work and family. "They see the senior women and they see the kinds of careers they have and it looks very unappealing to them. They want a career, but they want to be married and have kids. And they're willing to try to do both, but if they have to they will choose family over all."

What comes next? The class of 1990 promises to give corporations a major headache. We heard some rather astounding tales about the next generation of working people. Barney Olmsted of New Ways to Work tells of a call from a young man who was job-hunting. He wanted a list of companies with progressive parental leave policies, so he could be assured of time off when the time came. We met a thirty-year-old man who left his job at a nonprofit organization because he was not

---

A NEW ORGANIZATION MAN?

Some companies report that men attend parenting seminars, drop their children at day care, register just as much work/family stress as women on employee surveys, and even, in some cases, take parental leaves. But that depends on whom you're talking to. At Marriott Corporation, attendance at the parenting seminars is 50 percent male. At Johnson & Johnson, attendance at day-care meetings was only 10 percent male. At most companies, a handful of men—if any—take advantage of parental leave programs. And, with most men who take some time off to be with a newborn, it is generally taken in sick days, vacation time, or other paid leave time.

allowed time off to be with his newborn. Students are even asking campus recruiters about flexible options and reduced-hours policies during their job interviews. Says Jean Fraser, vice president of corporate relations at American Express: "This generation has caught on real fast. If they're comfortable enough asking about work/family benefits in an interview, they're going to be comfortable enough dealing with it later."

Hewitt Associates, a Chicago-based human resources consulting firm that recruits most of its new-hires right out of school, reports a rather dramatic shift in attitudes: "We have people coming in right out of school and one of the first things they say is, 'I don't want to be working a fifty-to-sixty-hour week. I want to find that balance in my life. I have interests outside of work. I may be getting married. I may or may not be having children that I want to spend time with.' They're willing

THE CORPORATION AS COMMUNITY

Employee Assistance Programs (EAPs) are one more way in which corporations play a supportive role in the lives of American parents. Considered a work/family benefit, EAPs are available at many progressive U.S. corporations. The services might include free referrals for alcohol or drug-abuse problems, help in finding a tutor for a learning-disabled child, and counseling.

Apple Computer uses cumulative data gathered through its counseling program to track changes in employee attitudes, although the company is quick to point out that information on individual employees is kept confidential.

At other firms, management training now means teaching supervisors how to deal with issues they didn't have to deal with fifteen or twenty years ago. Says one human resources executive: "A manager has to understand an employee's concerns, whether it's a baby being born or a teenager with psychiatric or drug-abuse problems or an elderly parent or a black experiencing discrimination or an Indonesian who doesn't understand American culture."

to talk about trade-offs pretty early in their careers." That's a tale we heard any number of times.

All of which suggests that the job applicants of the future will be asking questions like: Do you have on-site child care? What kind of benefits do you offer for job-sharers? What are the alternative career tracks at your company? What about the option of a part-time return following maternity leave? And, as a father, how long will my paid parental leave be?'

4

LEADERS IN
FLEXIBILITY

When we began this book in 1988, press clips furnished our early leads. What companies are promoting flexibility, we asked. We saw the same names mentioned again and again— Arthur Andersen, IBM, Merck & Co., and Time, Inc. When the subject was parental leave, there was IBM in the lead sentence. When job-sharing was the focus, Steelcase inevitably appeared in the piece. Either these companies have exceptional publicity machines, we thought, or there are only a few corporations allowing flexibility.

It turned out to be a little bit of both. On the one hand, the publicity value of work/family programs is not lost on some of these companies. For pacesetters like American Express and IBM, one of the motivations behind playing a leadership role is the desire to maintain that reputation. On the other hand, the pioneers deserve credit for being pioneers. Before 1988, when media attention really pushed work/family to the forefront, only a handful of companies had comprehensive programs that

51

dealt with a wide range of work/family issues. Today, thousands of companies offer at least one benefit related to the mutual needs of work and family. But how many offer flexibility?

INCREASES IN FLEXIBILITY

Flexibility is unquestionably on the rise. In 1989, the Conference Board released the most comprehensive survey to date of flexibility and corporate America. Of the 521 firms surveyed, about *one-third* had expanded their use of flextime, compressed work weeks, regular part-time, and job-sharing in recent years. Fully 486 offered some form of flexible scheduling or reduced work weeks.

The notion of flexible policies seems like an oxymoron. The more flexible a firm is, one would think, the less likely it is to have formal, written policies—rules governing hours, scheduling, where work is done, and when people can take time off. In trying to measure changing attitudes in American business, we looked first to major corporations *not* because we expected them to be more flexible than small businesses, but because big companies tend to institutionalize and legitimize change. They write policies down. They announce policy changes. Major corporations serve as barometers, not bellwethers. The fact that, by 1990, American corporations were beginning to address the issue of flexibility suggests that flexibility *is* becoming part of the American workplace. This is no short-term phenomenon. But it's worth noting that corporate policies affect very few people—only about 15 percent of the U.S. labor force works for major corporations. We see corporate flexibility as symptomatic of a broader change under way—in small business, professions, and government.

We collected information on more than 150 of the most progressive firms, a list culled from a variety of sources, including data gathered by the Families and Work Institute for its Corporate Reference Guide, information from business reporters in ten U.S. cities, and leads furnished by work/family consultants. We talked to more than fifty major corporations that offer some measure of flexibility, conducting in-depth interviews with thirty leading firms. What we found is this:

❑ Few companies are actually promoting flexible job arrangements, but a surprising number of large corporations are allowing, even expanding their flexible arrangements. Until very recently, a job-share worker or professional on a shortened work week had a very informal, privately negotiated arrangement. But major corporations are beginning to formalize alternative work schedule policies. US Sprint, Eastman Kodak, Merck and Co.,

---

A SLICE OF LIFE AT APPLE

Deborah Biondolillo, vice-president of human resources for Apple U.S.A., cut back to a four-day work week for six months during one stage of her career and found it stressful—because she couldn't get all her work done. "The flexibility was there and I had a very supportive manager, but there was too much work," she says. "We don't have a lot of extra people, so there wasn't anybody that I could hand the job to that didn't already have a hundred-percent job themselves." A company like Apple offers plenty of buffers against work/family stress—an outstanding on-site day-care facility, for example. It's unlikely that you'd have trouble taking time to care for a sick child or requesting personal time off. Technology helps. The voice mail system stands in for a missing receptionist or secretary. Every employee is provided with an Apple computer when they're hired (they own it once they've been on board a year), so work from home is possible in quite a few jobs. Says Biondolillo: "Between faxes and personal computers and networks and intermail systems and phone systems, you can be very productive without sitting in your office eight hours a day." But, although the company allows job-sharing, shorter hours, and work from home, it's difficult to imagine someone getting away with an alternative work-style that gives them real relief from the fast pace.

Corning, Aetna Life & Casualty, Honeywell, Steelcase, and Johnson & Johnson—to name just a few—all have *formal, written policies* governing job-sharing, part-time options, even work from home.

❑ At companies with flexible cultures—particularly young, entrepreneurial, hi-tech firms—flexibility has become a way of working. That's the up side. The down side is this: these fast-paced environments generally demand a commitment of more than eight hours a day. At Apple U.S.A., a division of Apple Computer, there are no set office hours. People come and go as they please. Still, Apple is a high-powered and lean organization; most people work *more,* not less, despite the flexibility.

Genentech, Inc., a South San Francisco biotechnology firm, has a similar corporate culture. There is no official parental leave policy. Instead, the company's disability leave program pays full salary for up to six months. Unpaid parental leave extends an additional six months. How much do most new mothers take at Genentech? An average of eight weeks.

Still, these companies offer a definite advantage. People are free to work at home. They can leave early to drive a car pool— and come back to work late. Says Linda Fitzpatrick, director of compensation, benefits, and systems at Genentech, "At the manager's discretion, anything's possible."

❑ The makeup of the part-time work force appears to be changing, spurring companies to rethink their policies. Take Digital Equipment Corporation's part-time work force as an example. Four years ago, the company had about 200 part-timers in its U.S. offices, most in administrative and clerical jobs. Today, there are 700 part-timers and job-sharers at Digital—the majority (475) hold salaried (not paid by the hour) managerial and professional jobs.

We found the same kind of mix at Hewlett-Packard, the giant maker of computational and measurement products, which recently completed a study of its part-time work force. Of the 585 regular part-timers, who are eligible for prorated benefits, merit pay increases, and profit-sharing, forty were supervisors and *more than half* were salaried employees. Says Quinn Kramer, an analyst in human resources who undertook the study: "We thought these would be the simplest jobs, the most routine functions. But we were wrong. Now we're looking at the question of what a manager does when a unit software engineer says she wants to go part-time. I think we get down on our hands and knees and say, 'What can we do to make you happy?' "

❑ Flexibility is there for the asking, particularly if you're considered a top performer. At most of the 150 firms we looked at, the prevailing attitude is this: "If an employee approaches us with a proposal, we'll consider it, but we're not going around soliciting job-shares or encouraging our managers to be more flexible." Only a handful of these leading-edge corporations told us they would *not* allow a valuable employee to cut back or share a job. In other words, many companies—even those that currently have no job-sharing or reduced work weeks—will bend the rules to accommodate a valuable employee.

❑ Naturally, some corporations are more enthusiastic than others. The top companies make an extra effort to be accommodating: by eliminating the obstacles that get in the way during negotiations, by training supervisors to be more flexible, by adding full-time staffers who serve as in-house consultants.

In Part III of this book, you'll find profiles of twenty-five leading companies with flexible policies. Some have outstanding parental leave programs; some lead in the area of sick care for kids; others promote alternative schedules. This listing is meant as a snapshot, outlining some of the best policies that exist in American corporations today. In compiling the list, we looked for the answers to these questions:

❑ Are you eliminating the barriers to flexibility?

❑ How many job-sharers and telecommuters do you have?

❑ Do you have employees on part-time schedules at the professional, technical, and managerial level?

❑ Are there pilot programs, experiments in job flexibility?

❏ Have you made an effort to publicize these policies on a corporation-wide basis?

❏ Do you post flexible jobs?

❏ Do you extend benefits to part-time people?

In considering which corporations offer flexibility, we were mindful of the differences between policies and practice. Companies *without* clear-cut policies are often the most flexible. And even in the most progressive companies, flexible policies must be translated through supervisors, managers, division heads, and operating groups. Reminds one work/family consultant: "For most people, it doesn't matter what the president thinks. It matters what their boss thinks."

The ten leading companies listed here have not only developed policies that encourage a wide range of flexible approaches, they've translated those policies into real flexibility. The evidence lies not only in their formal programs but in the number of people participating in those programs.

TEN OF THE MOST FLEXIBLE COMPANIES

Aetna Life & Casualty Co.
Bausch & Lomb
Corning*
Digital Equipment Corp.
Eastman Kodak Co.
Levi Strauss & Co.**
Northeast Utilities
Pioneer Hi-Bred International, Inc.
Steelcase, Inc.
US West

*Salaried employees only
**Employees on the headquarters payroll only

As we mentioned earlier, a number of companies that lead in implementing work/family benefits have put little or no emphasis on flexibility. At Group 243, a Michigan-based advertising firm with an outstanding work/family record, we were told that the high-powered advertising business leaves little room for flexibility. Although Group 243 allows special arrangements when it's necessary, there hasn't been much demand and power hours seem to prevail. At Syntex, a California-based company with a well-earned reputation for family-supportive policies, flexibility is not a priority and "no particular effort" is being made to encourage alternative arrangements, which are decided on a case-by-case basis. Merck & Co. is widely known as a leader in family-supportive programs; as of

---

THE *WORKING MOTHER* TOP TEN

Since 1986, *Working Mother* magazine has published an annual listing of the best companies for working mothers. In 1990, the list included 75 pacesetting firms with outstanding records for promoting women, paying competitive salaries, and offering work/family benefits. In 1990, the following companies were named to the *Working Mother* top ten.

Apple Computer
Beth Israel Hospital of Boston
Du Pont
Fel-Pro
Home Box Office
IBM
Merck & Co.
Morrison & Foerster
Procter & Gamble
SAS Institute

Reprinted by permission of Milton Moskowitz and Carol Townsend.

1990 the company was conducting its first and only job-share pilot involving two people. At Merck, flexibility has been introduced to middle-management jobs almost exclusively as an extension of maternity leaves. Still, such companies have outstanding supports for working parents—including progressive child care and parental leave policies.

What's holding up some of these otherwise progressive companies? For some, equity is a major concern. Companies that have across-the-board benefits programs and policies are hard-pressed to allow flexibility to a privileged few. Fel-Pro, a manufacturing company in Skokie, Illinois, consistently wins

CRUNCHING THE NUMBERS: OUR SOURCES AND RESOURCES

In 1988, when we began our research, few comprehensive studies of flexible jobs existed. The American Management Society (AMS) has been tracking part-time work and job-sharing since 1986 and temporary employment since 1977, providing the best comparative information on the market for flexible jobs. But beyond that, no one had published a comprehensive study of corporate flexibility. By 1989, three major research projects were nearing completion. In January 1990, the Conference Board released the results of a major study of flexible jobs among its member firms, conducted by Kathleen Christensen, director of the National Project for Home-Based Work in conjunction with New Ways to Work, the San Francisco research and consulting firm. Simultaneously, the Families and Work Institute was gathering data on work and family policies from more than 200 major corporations for a massive corporate reference guide, scheduled for publication in 1990. Catalyst, the New York–based consultant on women's issues, was finalizing its first study of flexible job-holders in major corporations. From these four studies, combined with our own research, our picture of corporate flexibility emerged.

plaudits for caring about its employees. The company has a summer camp, emergency in-home care for sick children (Fel-Pro foots part of the bill), and even a tutoring program for the learning-disabled children of employees. What about flexible jobs? "Flexibility," says Fel-Pro's communications manager Richard Morris, "is not the norm." Fel-Pro's concern is not an uncommon one. They feel that, in the interest of fairness, if they can't extend these policies to everyone, they are probably best left unexplored.

After all, the equity issue arises even in the most flexible companies. "Some managers think the best way to be equitable is to say no to everybody. Then they can never be accused of discriminating," says Sherry Herchenroether, who manages Aetna's work/family programs. It's not surprising that some of the most successful programs include clear guidelines for selecting the candidates for flexibility. Northeast Utilities, the Connecticut-based power company, provides a complete package for prospective job-sharers, including a self-appraisal form, checklist of issues to consider, a job-sharing agreement, and job analysis sheet to help job-sharers divvy up responsibilities. US West publishes guidelines for prospective telecommuters in order to syphon qualified employees into their telecommuting program—and to send a clear signal to those who don't qualify.

Then there's the floodgate issue: *if we let one person do it, everyone will want to do it.* But the fact is, not everyone can afford a flexible job. And not everyone wants to work at home or shorten their schedule. At Corning, where all 6,000 salaried employees are technically eligible for flexible options, only forty are participating. At Steelcase, Inc., the Michigan-based furniture manufacturer, which has offered job-sharing since 1982, out of more than 8,000 eligible employees, only ninety-four people are job-sharers. Says Joe Pearce, employee relations manager, "What we're seeing over time is that the numbers stay the same, but the people keep changing." Steelcase's experience suggests that people use flexibility as a short-term option, scaling back for a time, then returning to a full-time level.

Even at accommodating companies, resistance to flexibility is sometimes built into the system. Common holdups to successful negotiations include benefits and headcount policies.

When budgets, productivity measures, and evaluations are based on headcounts, managers are loath to explore alternative schedules or job-shares if a part-timer counts the same as a full-timer. Aetna Life & Casualty recently changed its headcount system so a part-time person is counted as just that—but it took nearly four years to implement the change.

Often, people who work fewer than thirty or forty hours a week have been ineligible for health benefits. American Express changed its benefits policies in January 1989 so part-timers could receive full-time benefits. Sometimes the process works in reverse: to encourage flexibility, some companies change the benefits rules so that part-timers *are no longer* eligible for full-time benefits—introducing, instead, prorated benefits for part-timers.

THE QUESTION OF BENEFITS

At the very least, equitable treatment of part-timers means access to prorated benefits and the ability to buy into full health insurance coverage. Companies that offer *full* health benefits to part-time people have found that only about 50 percent take advantage of medical coverage. More than three-quarters of the Conference Board companies surveyed offered some form of benefits coverage to part-timers and more than half offer the same health benefits to part- and full-time people.

The ultimate holdup to increased flexibility is attitude. Here are the questions we heard over and over:

❑ How do you make shortened hours, job-sharing, and tele-commuting work?

❑ Don't flexible jobs mean more work for supervisors?

❑ How do you evaluate job-sharing pairs?

❑ How do you split the responsibilities?

❑ How do you supervise people who work at home?

❑ How do you turn full-time jobs into half-time ones?

The concept of flexibility challenges some dearly held assumptions about work—how it's done and how much time it takes. Do people stretch the job to fit the time? Can one job be split efficiently into two part-time jobs? Are people on reduced schedules more productive? These are the kinds of issues the consultants are grappling with.

They maintain that attitude is everything. Consider this tale, told by Cecile Klavens, president of the Pickwick Group, a Massachusetts-based placement firm specializing in professionals and executives on alternative schedules. She did a study of two identical departments at two Boston-area banks. At one, job-sharing had been integrated into departmental operations and was going smoothly; in fact, it was a *solid* success. At the same department at the other bank, management maintained that job-sharing would be impossible because of the nature of

---

JOB-SHARING: STRAIGHT FACTS

❑ The Conference Board study found that *four out of five job-sharing pairs are in administrative support or clerical jobs.*

❑ Less than one-fifth of the companies surveyed (98 out of 521) offer job-sharing.

❑ The vast majority of job-shares are *ad hoc,* individually negotiated, specially arranged. Fewer than one third (29 percent) of those ninety-eight companies have written job-sharing policies.

❑ At the companies that have job-sharing, the median number of job-sharing pairs in place is *two to three pairs.*

❑ We found only one job-sharing pair at the vice-president level—at Manufacturers Hanover—and only a handful of job-shares at the director level.

the work. In fact, says Klavens, the functions in the two bank departments were identical. The only difference was that one had job-sharing and one didn't. Attitude was the holdup at bank number two. Says Klavens: "The success of these arrangements really has more to do with motivation than anything else."

If you are interested in exploring the how-tos of flexibility, we recommend *Creating a Flexible Workplace: How to Select and Manage Alternative Work Options* (see Bibliography), by Barney Olmsted and Suzanne Smith of New Ways to Work. It is a practical guide to designing and managing more flexible work arrangements.

BEYOND CORPORATE AMERICA: FINDING FLEXIBILITY IN GOVERNMENT

The walls are a glossy white, framing a series of small, oblong offices with built-in bookcases and laminated desktops. Though filled with books, art, and personal mementoes, these rooms have an uncluttered feel about them, a streamlined hominess. Each is equipped with a computer. They open up to a long, central space, framed in glass, overlooking a massive atrium, a triple-height space with walls that must stretch fifty feet above the floor. These might be the offices of an architect or an editor. But this is a government office, one that betrays the image of a graying, file-cabinet-filled haven for bureaucrats. The atrium is, in fact, a library and the employees that work here work for the federal government. This is the Cataloging Section of the National Gallery of Art Library.

Five years ago, when Jane Collins headed up this office, she approached her boss about stepping down. She wanted to give up her supervisory responsibilities, cut back to a twenty-hour work week, and enroll in a landscape architecture program. She was ready for a midlife career change. Collins, a straightforward and practical sort, had a contingency plan. If the National Gallery refused her request, she would apply for a post as a gardener at the gallery itself. But, with ten years tenure and the top post in a department of professionals, Collins would have been taking ten steps back to move one step forward. She didn't have to. The gallery accepted her plan.

Since then, the cataloging department has been transformed into a model of flexibility. Here's how the current supervisor, Roger Lawson, describes the five staffers who hold the three positions on the staff: "Jane and Gail share a job. Gail also has eight hours of Cathy's job. So Jane works twenty hours, Cathy works thirty-two, Gail works twenty-eight. Marsha and Trudi each work twenty hours." In other words, Lawson, who is himself on flextime, supervises three part-timers and two job-sharers, as well as two temporary technicians. A nightmare? Not to hear Roger Lawson tell it.

HOW WIDESPREAD IS FLEXTIME?

Nearly half of the Conference Board companies that offer some kind of flexibility offer flextime. Of these, a little over half (54 percent) have formal policies or written guidelines for flextime. The AMS study of smaller firms found 30 percent offer flextime, up from 15 percent in 1977. We found that the most progressive companies are being more flexible about flextime. The core hours—the times when people are required to be at their desks—seems to be shrinking. That gives working parents more flexibility. At Champion International, a Connecticut-based paper company, the core hours are 10 A.M. to 2 P.M. That means a parent could potentially come to work at 7 A.M. and leave at 3 P.M., not a bad schedule for someone who has a spouse to handle the morning routine and does an after-school pickup at 3:15.

Cataloging books, a profession requiring a master's degree in library science, is a self-contained, self-directed process. People work independently, although overlapping time has been created for a weekly staff meeting when necessary. The flexible approach means Lawson has to do more performance appraisals; his administrative load is greater. But he has nothing but positive things to say about the whole arrangement. After all, when Roger Lawson joined the department, Jane Collins was his boss, everyone was full-time, and he was a technician. The reshuffling not only enabled Collins to pursue her new career, it has opened a path for Lawson's career growth and created what to all appearances is one, big, very happy family. "I think this speaks to the success of the department," says Lawson. "Nobody wants to leave."

There are a number of lessons to be learned from the National Gallery's cataloging staff. For one thing, output for a cataloger is easily measured, so they have reliable productivity numbers. Overall, the department catalogs 5,000 titles a year. Productivity for the former full-timers has remained the same. For another, it speaks to the fact that even in the federal government, that vast bureaucratic machine, flexibility thrives.

In fact, the government is emerging as a leader in flexibility. It's difficult to say just how widespread flexibility has become, because, in truth, the government itself doesn't know. When we talked to the federal administrator in charge of alternative schedules, she was trying to find job-sharing pairs in government work to hold up as examples to encourage *more* job-sharing. Unfortunately, they were hidden in the statistics on part-time work. We found numerous people in job-shares, on flexible schedules, flextime, and reduced work weeks in a variety of jobs throughout the federal government. Aside from flextime schedules, every arrangement we found had been privately negotiated between an employee and his or her boss.

The federal government is in the process of clarifying its personnel policies to open the way for more flexibility, no easy task for a bureaucracy that encompasses fourteen departments, 120 agencies, and 2.2 million employees throughout the United States. In 1989, a "Flexiplace Task Force" was sponsored by the President's Council on Management Improvement. Its goal: to make it easier for people to telecommute by eliminating some of the bureaucratic and policy holdups to such arrangements. According to Wendell Joice, codirector of the task force: "A lot of agencies have telecommuting on an individual basis, but they would worry about the legalities and technicalities"—issues like liability coverage for people working from home and how to handle pay rates if an employee's house is outside the bounds of a geographical jurisdiction. In 1989, the task force published telecommuting guidelines for supervisors and began the process of soliciting agencies for a pilot program. The next step: training sessions and follow-up focus groups. "Recruiting," says Joice, "is the major issue. Government has difficulty recruiting strictly on the basis of salaries. But if you start adding goodies, then you increase your ability to attract new recruits."

Some local governments, particularly those that compete in tight or progressive labor markets, have become very flexible. Minneapolis and Milwaukee have both earned publicity for their progressive workplace reforms. In 1989, Milwaukee's entire civil service code was being rewritten to incorporate more flexibility, including flextime, a six-month parental leave policy, compressed work weeks, and job-sharing. At that time, 110 city employees were on half-time schedules. According to the *New York Times*, competition for employees was the key to Milwaukee's workplace reforms, where unemployment was at 4 percent in 1989.

There are heartening signs of progress at the state level as well. California has a pilot telecommuting program under way,

---

TELECOMMUTING: NOT FOR WOMEN ONLY

Telecommuting is a different animal. Most people on alternative schedules are women. Not so telecommuters: most are men. And most work full-time. The motivations behind telecommuting have more to do with cost savings, productivity, and avoiding a commute than the desire to spend more time at home. In fact, Catalyst's study revealed that only 30 percent of telecommuters were working at home to spend more time with their families. Few telecommuters spend every day at home; most are required to come into the office at least one day a week. Recent research has shattered another myth about telecommuting: the only equipment most telecommuters use to communicate with the office is a telephone.

as does the Washington State Energy Office. New York State reportedly posts job-shares. Massachusetts, which passed legislation on alternative work schedules in the 1970s, has seen a dramatic rise in alternative scheduling during the eighties. Although the department that administers alternative work schedules was abolished with the state's dramatic 1989 budget cuts, it had apparently achieved some results. In 1989, there were 65,000 state employees in the executive branch. Of those, nearly 14,000 were on flextime or staggered hours (up from 3,000 to 4,000 six years ago) and 5,000 work part-time (up from 2,000 six years ago.)

Still, an employee is just as likely to encounter resistance to flexibility in a government job as in a corporate one. It's all a matter of where you work, whom you work for, and what you do.

5

FLEXIBILITY, EQUALITY, MATERNITY: WHERE TO FROM HERE?

MATERNITY LEAVE: A SPECIAL CASE FOR FLEXIBILITY

The issue of maternity leave, now often referred to as parental leave, is a very personal one. Not long ago, I, Susan, met a dentist, a good-natured woman with two children born eighteen months apart. Hers is a private practice, and until very recently, she was it—the only dentist in the office. I thought I'd heard all the maternity leave stories imaginable until I heard hers. She took two days off to have her first baby and two days off to have her second. "What choice did I have?" she asks rhetorically. "What was I supposed to tell my patients? I'm sorry you're in pain, but I just had a baby. I can't help you." Her attitude was pretty straightforward: you do what you gotta do. "You put it on autopilot," she said. "And you just keep going."

Is two days enough time for most women? Probably not.

What about twelve weeks? Consider this account from a first-time mother in her mid-twenties who returned to work twelve weeks after her daughter was born. "I went back to work when my daughter was three months old. I can remember several weeks when she was really agitated every evening for a few hours after I'd pick her up at the sitter's. But, if it's your first child, you don't know whether that's just a normal stage of infancy or the baby's personality or something has gone on that day," she says. "I was really worried. So one day, when I had gone to pick her up and I wasn't thinking, I was speeding through a school zone. This policeman stopped me and I just started sobbing. I said, 'I can't believe you're doing this to me. I just picked up my daughter. And I'm trying to work and take care of this baby. And I think something's wrong.' He just looked at me like I was crazy. But it was all this built-up tension just coming out."

Even under ideal conditions—where baby and mother are both healthy—working full-time and having a newborn isn't anybody's idea of a good time. Different people respond differently to the combined joys and stresses of giving birth, caring for a new baby, hiring a caregiver or finding day care, and leaving that baby to go back to work. At eight weeks, it's a rare mother who can hop right into a dress-for-success wardrobe. Even at twelve weeks, most parents aren't getting a full night's sleep every night.

In truth, recent studies tell us that most women are not ready to go back to work full-time in five weeks, eight weeks, even twelve weeks. One in-depth study of 181 new mothers cited in *The Parental Leave Crisis* found that most women are physically ready to go back to work after three months, but they're not emotionally ready for six months. Based on the responses of focus groups at major corporations, Fran Rodgers, president of Work/Family Directions, maintains that most women want a three- to six-month leave, plus the option of a gradual or part-time return. Says Rodgers: "The worst thing is when people are forced to go back full-time after six weeks or even twelve weeks. They're tired, they're still feeling pulled, and it's just not a very realistic approach for any human being."

Liberal parental leave policies may be the single most important vehicle for keeping women in the labor force. Why?

❑ We were surprised, perhaps naively, to find that most of the women we interviewed made the switch to a more flexible job shortly after having a baby. Most of them would have quit otherwise. An enlightened parental leave policy could very well mean the difference between losing and keeping that employee.

❑ Our findings were confirmed by a recent study conducted by the research group Catalyst. They found that one-third of the women with flexible jobs "would not or could not have returned to work after having a child" had they not had a flexible alternative.

❑ Companies that introduce a part-time return option have found that such programs increase the likelihood that new mothers will not only return to work but remain employed long-term.

❑ The National Council of Jewish Women Center for The Child found that new mothers who work for accommodating companies and supportive supervisors are more likely to come back to

---

ON THE RISE: NEW MOTHERS IN THE WORK FORCE

The fastest-growing group of working mothers in today's labor force are those with children under the age of one year. In 1987, 51 percent of the mothers with children under the age of one were employed, as opposed to 24 percent in 1970 and 19 percent in 1960. Women are also having children later, when they are more likely to be established in their careers and more valuable to their employers.

work. Their study of more than 2,000 working women found that 78 percent of those in "highly accommodating" workplaces returned to their employers—versus 50 percent of those in "nonaccommodating" situations.

Having a new baby, however uplifting, can be stressful. Because it's so personal, it's a time when parents most need options. From a business standpoint, the question is this: Why risk losing a valuable employee to inflexible leave policies? From a broader perspective, though, the issue is this: How much time does a new baby need to spend with its mother? And how much time do new mothers need to spend with their babies?

Herein lies the rub: just when many companies thought it was safe to offer a paid leave that could be stretched to three or four months, and to assume that a happy compromise between business needs and baby's needs had been reached, along came the attachment theorists. These are the folks who believe that mother-child bonding during the first year of life is the single, most critical factor in determining the future security and well-being of a child.

Popularized by T. Berry Brazelton, M.D., a latter-day Dr. Spock whose approach is rooted in attachment theory, this notion of the importance of early bonding makes a strong case for in-home care during infancy and an even stronger case for maternal care. A number of attachment theorists have produced some profoundly damning studies of day care, particularly infant day care. According to a report in *The Atlantic,* Mary Ainsworth, a researcher who pioneered attachment studies, maintains that it's not necessary for a mother to be present *all the time,* but it helps if she's a "constant presence" in the child's life. After all, Ainsworth and her colleagues maintain, it's a sensitive mother who sets the stage for a child's healthy emotional development, his or her sense that all's well with the world.

Children who lack that sense of security, according to this view, develop learning problems, behavior problems, and, not surprisingly, attachment problems. From an article by Robert Karen in the February 1990 issue of *The Atlantic* comes this political hot potato: " 'It's very hard to become a sensitive, responsive mother if you're away from your child ten hours a day,' says Ainsworth. 'It really is.' " The most radical attachment theorist, Jay Belsky of the University of Pennsylvania, maintains that a mother's absence for more than twenty hours a week, when a child is under a year of age, puts that child at risk.

Whether attachment theorists are correct or not is arguable. Regardless, the rising interest in attachment theory could raise the guilt level of working mothers to an all-time high. But perhaps, instead, the discussion will lead us to reconsider our goals as a society. If women are in the work force to stay, it is time to develop realistic, workable parental leave policies— policies that give new parents time to take care of their business at home. After all, the parental leave issue is not just a *short-term* business concern. We have the security, productivity, and employability of each successive generation to consider.

How much time, then? The problem is this: it's not just a question of time, or rather, time off. It's a question of how much time off *with pay*. How much time off *with a job guarantee*? How much time off with employee-paid health insurance coverage? How much additional time off without pay—that is, unpaid leave? And what about the possibility of returning on a reduced schedule?

We think the best solution from the standpoint of employer, employee, and child is an eight- to twelve-week paid leave plus the option of a phased part-time return to work.

ADOPTION AID

A family benefit offered by leading-edge companies is adoption assistance in the form of money to defray the costs of adopting a child. The amounts range from $500 to $3,000, the most generous figure we encountered. Truly progressive companies also offer paid leave time to adoptive parents and extend their unpaid parental leaves to adoptive parents.

That's hardly an outrageous proposal. In Europe, *a six-month leave with pay,* followed by additional unpaid leave time, is available in many countries. The Maternity Protection Recommendation, ratified by eighteen European countries more than twenty-five years ago, calls for a fourteen-week job-protected leave at 100 percent of a woman's salary, with her seniority remaining intact.

In 1990, the U.S. Congress passed legislation requiring employers with fifty or more employees to provide an *unpaid,* job-guaranteed leave of up to twelve weeks for birth or adoption, as well as cases of serious illness. President Bush vetoed the bill in early July. As a result, the United States remains the only industrialized country without a national family leave policy.

What benefits currently exist in the United States? In 1987, the National Council of Jewish Women (NCJW) released the results of one of the most comprehensive studies of parental leaves ever undertaken. The sample included more than 2,200 companies and organizations—representing all sizes and industries and covering more than 2 million women. The survey, conducted by the NCJW Center for the Child, covered five key benefits and found that *only 3 percent* of all employers, large or small, offered all five of these programs—widely considered the critical elements of an enlighted parental leave policy:

❏ A job-protected medical leave of eight weeks or more

❏ Employer contribution to health insurance during that leave

❏ Some wage or salary replacement during the leave

❏ The option of additional unpaid time off following the eight-week leave

❏ The ability to come back part-time following the eight-week leave

Entire books have been written on the subject of parental leave. Reams of Congressional testimony have been prepared on the subject. Exhaustive studies have been conducted. Still, it's difficult to tell just what's out there and who's covered by what. The U.S. Bureau of Labor Statistics maintains that every employee of a large or medium-sized business is covered by some kind of paid, short-term sick or disability leave policy. But "short-term" could mean as little as ten days' or as much as nine months' coverage.

A paid, job-protected six- to eight-week maternity leave or, rather, disability leave, is considered the norm in American business. But that is by no means available universally. Some studies have found that, across all industries, only 40 percent of all working women are eligible for any kind of job-guaranteed leave with pay.

Major corporations offer the best benefits. According to a 1986 study by Catalyst, 90 percent of the Fortune 500 firms surveyed provided leave with *some* pay and continued medical benefits. Many women who work for big companies are able to put together a three-month paid leave by combining accrued vacation time, sick leave, and disability leave.

In recent years, large companies have expanded their un-paid leave policies, creating parental and family-leave programs that may stretch up to a year. In the case of *parental* leaves, men are eligible. In the case of *family* leave, almost any family-related emergency qualifies as a reasonable cause for leave. Based on our discussions with these companies, most people don't take full advantage of these programs, because they can't afford to take twelve, ten, or even two months off without pay. That's why the option of a part-time return becomes critical.

The International Business Machines (IBM) policy is widely considered the standard against which all parental leave policies are measured. In addition to a six- to eight-week paid disability leave, new parents can take up to three years' unpaid leave—with an employment guarantee and restoration of sen-iority upon return. During that three-year period, the company pays full benefits. Employees have the option of working a flexible or shortened schedule at any time during that three years, and they're required to be available for part-time work during years two and three.

We think the most appealing aspect of the IBM policy is the part-time return option. In fact, more and more companies are allowing women to come back part-time following a maternity leave. Often it's up to a supervisor's discretion. But we found scores of major corporations open to that possibility.

THE PART-TIME RETURN OPTION

Increasingly, major employers are allowing special arrangements that enable new mothers to return to work part-time following a maternity leave. According to one study by Catalyst, 60 percent of surveyed Fortune 500 corporations make such options available. In every case, the arrangement must be agreeable to the supervisor and suit the particular needs of a job. Listed below are some of the companies that allow the part-time return option. In some cases, eligibility is limited to salaried, nonunion, or headquarters employees.

Aetna Life & Casualty
Allstate Insurance Co.
American Cyanamid Co.
American Express Co.
American Greetings Corp.
American Information
  Technologies Corporation
  (Ameritech)
Arthur Andersen & Co.
Delta Air Lines, Inc.
Deluxe Corp.
Digital Equipment Corp.
Dow Chemical, USA
Du Pont Co.
Eastman Kodak Co.
Exxon Corp.
Gannett Co., Inc.
Hallmark Cards, Inc.
Hechinger Co.
Herman Miller, Inc.
Hewlett-Packard Co.

Honeywell, Inc.
IBM
Johnson & Johnson
Knight-Ridder, Inc.
Lockheed Corp.
McGraw-Hill, Inc.
Merck & Co., Inc.
Metropolitan Life Insurance Co.
Minnesota Mining &
  Manufacturing Co. (3M)
Mobil Corp.
Nynex Corp.
Pacific Gas & Electric Co.
Pacific Telesis Group
Sears, Roebuck and Co.
Textron, Inc.
Time Inc. Magazines
Travelers Insurance Co.
US Sprint
U S West, Inc.
Warner-Lambert Co.
Xerox Corp.

Based on data collected by the Families and Work Institute for *The Corporate Reference Guide* as well as on our research.

CREATIVE SOLUTIONS

Jan Honeycutt is the curator of exhibits at a West Coast museum. Hers is a high-level government job. Eight years ago, when Honeycutt had her first child, she became the first woman in her department ever to take a maternity leave. After a four-month leave, she made special arrangements to return to work two days a week. Several months later, she escalated to a three-day work week. Then, after a year, she was back full-time. She negotiated a similar schedule when her second son was born in 1984. Her situation is not unique. It's only been in the last ten or fifteen years that U.S. employers have had to grapple with the issue of maternity leave on a *large scale and at all levels in an organization.* Given that, employers have come up with some creative solutions to leave-taking.

TEMPORARY TELECOMMUTERS

We found scores of companies where flexible jobs are open almost exclusively to women who've just taken a maternity leave. Increasingly, women are allowed to work from home. A study by Catalyst found that 22 percent of human resources managers surveyed use work-from-home as an alternative for women on maternity leave.

The 1980s may well be remembered as the era when women took outrageously short maternity leaves. This tale, recounted in a book entitled *The Best Companies for Women*, typifies the attitude and behavior of many career-minded women, when faced with the prospect of staying on the fast track and having a baby: Ann Moore, a general manager at *Sports Illustrated*, attended an out-of-town business meeting two and a half weeks after her son was born and went back to work full-time five and a half weeks later. That, despite the fact that Time Inc. Magazines, *Sports Illustrated*'s parent company, allows up to a year off without pay. Moore told the authors: "Certainly it's a little insulting to imagine that we can go without a general manager for a year. Or a publisher. If women want equality, start admitting there's a price you pay for it." We wonder how high a price women should be willing to pay for the right to keep their jobs, to be productive members of society, to make a contribution?

We applaud any effort to give women more leeway after they've had a baby. But, in looking more closely at some of the new, creative approaches to leave, our fear is that one set of unrealistic expectations will replace another.

Consider this example: at Johnson & Johnson, the company's in-house publication pictures a woman sitting at her desk, working full-time from home, with a baby in the background. That is Johnson & Johnson's way of signaling supervisors to bend a little, to be creative in accommodating talented women. As such, it is a symbol of a new corporate attitude. But the sad truth is that the picture is no more realistic than the Superwoman image of the seventies—that infamous model for the Enjoli commercial who brought home the bacon and fried

---

BEST UNPAID LEAVE PROGRAM: U S WEST

At US West, taking a year off without pay is not as risky as it is at most companies. For up to twelve months, the company *continues all benefits and pays 100 percent of all normal health coverage.* That includes tuition assistance, which means employees can take time off to go to school without giving up their medical and dental coverage or death benefits. Reinstatement in a comparable job—and in some departments, the same job—is guaranteed. Employees are even allowed to work for someone else during the leave, provided it's not a U S West competitor. Beyond that, employees can petition to extend such leaves for twelve additional months.

US West launched this new "enhanced leave" policy in 1990 for infant care, family care, or other personal reasons, and recommended its adoption in all forty of the company's divisions and subsidiaries—so 65,000 employees are potentially eligible for the program.

it up in the pan. The truth is, it's nearly impossible to take care of children and do a full-time job from home. Most consultants and companies urge telecommuters to find child care if they're going to work at home. The idea of watching baby and minding the store—at the same time—is a formula for failure. Such arrangements are no more realistic than expecting women to go to business meetings two weeks after giving birth.

FOR FACTS ABOUT PARENTAL LEAVE

For a closer look at parental leave policies—past, present, and future—we suggest *The Parental Leave Crisis: Toward a National Policy*, edited by Edward F. Zigler and Meryl Frank (Yale University Press: New Haven, 1988).

NEW TWISTS ON JOB FLEXIBILITY:
LOOKING AT THINGS FROM ANOTHER ANGLE

A number of our findings surprised us: the extent to which corporations have begun to formalize flexibility, the degree to which women have pushed for change, and a general willingness to bend to the needs of *new* mothers. But numerous issues, some of which relate to the direction flexibility will take in the future, perplexed or intrigued us. Here are a few of them.

What about recruiting? Given the fact that so many businesses are becoming more flexible to attract and retain good people, we expected more companies to be using flexibility as a recruiting tool. Evidence suggests that there are vast numbers of women out there who want to work part-time. A 1986 Gallup poll revealed that *71 percent of at-home mothers would like to work.* And, while women continue to go into business for themselves in record numbers, many of these businesses are hardly booming: 54 percent of the firms owned by nonminority women had receipts or sales of less than $5,000 in 1982. Is there a legitimate place for such women in American business—in the form of secure but flexible careers with access to benefits, career growth, training, and promotions?

We met a woman named Dorothy Hevey at a work/family conference. An EEO consultant at GE Information Services in Rockville, Maryland, she had plans to tap into this market by advertising for area people interested in alternative schedules. These would not be second-rate jobs, spots in the contingent labor pool, but genuine career opportunities with shorter hours. Her proposal is still just that—in the proposal stages. But to us, Hevey sounds like someone on the leading edge. What better way to deal with the labor shortage than to draw on this supply of motivated, educated women who want career challenges and flexibility?

Of course, not everyone sees things that way. When we asked one advocate of flexibility, a corporate human resources consultant whose offices are not far from Hevey's, about developing corporate job-sharing, she had this to say: "If you're having difficulty recruiting people, then job-sharing is not much of an option, because you have to find *two* people instead of one." That, we think, misses the point. Finding two job-sharers—two qualified people willing to work shorter hours—could be easier than finding a full-timer in today's job market. But that, it appears, is not the consensus view.

In our minds, it's unlikely that businesses will successfully confront the problems raised by a changing labor market until they begin to think in new and untraditional ways about who can do what jobs and how work gets done.

Hiring temporary professionals and managers is one twist on the recruiting theme. In the fields of law and accounting, an increasing number of temporary agencies serve as clearing-houses for professionals who don't want to work full-time. Some of the Big Eight accounting firms actively recruit former employees to help out during the tax season. Even executives and managers are joining the temporary labor market. But the idea of actively recruiting permanent, salaried careerists on reduced schedules is still quite rare. In fact, some companies require employees to have a year's tenure before considering them for a part-time slot.

The Daddy Track. We looked long and hard for evidence that men are opting for flexibility, particularly after reading a spate of articles that came out in 1989 and 1990 on the subject. We found almost none. At Steelcase, seven men hold flexible jobs. At most companies, though, the number was closer to zero. Generally, men take flexible jobs for work-related, not family-related reasons—in other words, they're not on the Daddy Track, they're just on a different track. The field of architecture abounds with examples. It's not uncommon for architecture professors to be practicing architects. As a result, many architects—men and women—teach part-time and practice part-time. Some have been known to do *both* full-time. Thomas Beeby, dean of the Yale architecture school in New Haven, Connecticut, has a thriving private practice halfway across the country in Chicago. That kind of flexibility is motivated by professional, not family, considerations.

We did, however, find a disproportionate number of Daddy Trackers among journalists. Journalism may well be the most flexible profession, in part because of the nature of the work. Reporters generate a tangible, measurable product. An article or column produced from home is ample evidence that the writer did not spend the day at the beach. In journalism, we found not just job-sharing pairs, but job-sharing teams. Three women at the *Seattle Times* share a single reporting slot in the news features department. Two women share a research job at a local bureau of the *New York Times;* a third member of the team fills in as needed. At the moment, the environmental reporters on the Washington staff of the *Wall Street Journal* are job-sharers. We found a slew of alternative arrangements, including part-time reporter slots, at the *Des Moines Register* and the *Kansas City Star.* Undoubtedly, there are plenty more out there. In 1989, the *Seattle Times* incorporated job-sharing into its union agreement with the Pacific Northwest Newspaper Guild—as far as we know, the first paper to do so.

Most interesting, though, is the extent to which men are participating in some of these arrangements. Job-sharing marriages are not unheard of in the news business. William and Margaret Freilvogel share the post of assistant Washington bureau chief for the *St. Louis Post-Dispatch.* Will Englund and Kathy Lally share a reporter slot at the *Baltimore Sun.* We encountered one couple actively involved in a nationwide search for a reporter's job to share—and a dozen newspapers throughout the country were willing to explore the possibility. In each of these cases, the motivation behind flexibility was family-, not job-related. These fathers are sharing in child care. And, if a Daddy Track exists, they are indeed on it.

Lifestylers. We also encountered a group we'll call lifestylers—people who opt for flexibility to pursue some hobby, interest, or obsession. An Atlanta reporter put us on the track of a pair of white-water canoeists who are trying to balance work and canoeing. We found a pediatrician who worked a reduced schedule so she could travel. A number of companies told us that their alternative schedules were designed, not just with parents in mind, but to accommodate people who wanted to write the great American novel or sail around the world. But the truth is, statistically, that most holders of flexible jobs are women and most are mothers. It's a rare soul who can afford to take time off to sail around the world. Nice idea, though!

Retraining. More common are the part-timers who cut back to go to school. Retraining is a compelling, and rarely cited, reason for introducing flexibility. Nearly one-quarter of the employees studied in the Boston University Job and Homelife Study attend school outside of work. "When you look at the projections for the educational level of the work force by the year 2000, you're talking about some real problem areas," says Barney Olmsted, co-author of *Creating a Flexible Workplace*. "Part-time not only means you can combine work and family life, it means you can combine work with education." That's an angle that has gone relatively unexplored at American corporations—and one that, with a little creative thinking, could potentially extend the benefits of flexibility to more people.

FLEXIBILITY AND THE PROFESSIONAL TRACK

The concept of a "mommy track"—a separate and unequal career path for mothers who want flexibility—really originated in the nation's law firms. The day they're hired, lawyers in major firms move onto a rigidly prescribed track leading to the rank of partner. Typically, that means working long, hard hours—ten, twelve, fourteen hours a day, weekends at the office, vacations on the phone or at the fax. There's also a prescribed timeline tied to making partner. In most law firms, if you're not named partner within seven to ten years, you're not going to become a partner and you're expected to leave the firm. But women are beginning to change all that.

Twenty percent of American lawyers are now women and some of these women have been unwilling to work eighty hours a week. Here's the problem: if a lawyer isn't on the partner track, it throws everything out of whack—salaries, rank, bonuses, everything is tied into a track. In a law firm, getting off the fast track challenges the system on which the entire hierarchy is based. So, law firms are coming up with new titles, new salary structures, new approaches for top performers who want to scale back. Typically, a lawyer who scales back before he or she becomes a partner is either out of the running for partner or considerably slowed down in his or her quest for partnership. At Morrison & Foerster, one of the most progressive firms in the country, which offers job-sharing, staggered hours, and other flexible options to staff members, this is the policy regarding flexible hours for attorneys: "Flexible work arrangements may be approved for lawyer personnel for the purpose of devoting time to the raising of children. A reduction in compensation must be agreed upon; an associate's progress toward partnership will be delayed." That's a *liberal* policy; in some firms, partnership is no longer an option.

As you'll see in Part II, some lawyers working with major firms have negotiated workable part-time arrangements. We found that the success of these arrangements depends largely on supportive colleagues, attitudes at the office, and a lawyer's relationship with her clients. We found, too, that lawyers who work for government, for small firms, even in corporate offices are more likely to reach a happy compromise than are those in large firms. Why? Because working for a large law firm has always been, by its very nature, a fast-track occupation. Long hours are part of how the game is played. Among major law firms, the most popular work/family benefit seems to be emergency child care and care for sick children—policies that enable people to keep working no matter what kind of crisis arises at home. These are essential policies for a family-supportive workplace, because, as we all know, sometimes no matter what happens at home, you've got to be at work. But, taken alone, such programs are symbolic of a fast-track mentality that in itself can put stress on working parents.

Accounting is not unlike law, and women have invaded the field. The job itself is largely based on client service, professionals are on a prescribed career track (it generally takes between eleven and thirteen years to make partner), and large firms dominate the field. In 1989, in response to a rising interest in alternative scheduling, the American Woman's Society of Certified Public Accountants (AWSCPA) did a major study of flexibility in the accounting field. They found flexible arrangements at all the major accounting firms—generally referred to as the Big Eight—and a growing willingness to be flexible among all types of firms. The most interesting finding was this: despite the fact that most women accountants expected flexibility to hurt their careers, opting for flexibility, in fact, caused very little career damage. Two-thirds of the women accountants with flexible jobs did not feel they were penalized in terms of salary, benefits, or status when they scaled back or went on a flexible schedule.

Like law firms, accounting firms are trying to come up with solutions to the flexibility issue. Arthur Andersen, the largest accounting and management consulting firm in the world, has one of the best parental leave policies in American business. In addition to a paid disability leave of up to ninety days (depending on years of service), the firm grants up to twelve months of unpaid leave. Beyond that, accountants have the option of returning to work on a flexible schedule or shorter hours for up to three years after birth or adoption. Called the "Flexible Work Program for Managers," the part-time return option is designed for manager-level accountants, most of whom reach manager in their mid- to late twenties. "We've found that, in the generation coming up, women are having children when they are between the ages of twenty-six and twenty-eight. They do it at the manager level, when they've got more control of their time," says Peter Pesce, managing director of human resources. To date, about a hundred managers and more than half of Arthur Andersen's seventy-five offices are experimenting with the part-time option. According to Pesce, a dozen offices were already following such flexibility before the formal program was introduced. The company is in the process of redefining the partner track itself and looking closely at flexible options, including a broader range of titles.

Management consulting firms operate much like professional firms. Hewitt Associates, a management consulting firm with twenty-four U.S. offices and twenty-six outside the U.S., has a slew of progressive work/family policies. That's not surprising, given that the company advises other businesses on compensation and benefits issues. In addition, more than half of Hewitt's professional staff is made up of women; the average age is twenty-nine to thirty. The driving force behind these programs is a desire to support these people so that they can balance home and work—on a full-time schedule. "Our approach has been to support our associates being in the workplace full-time," says Dave Wille, who heads the human resources function at Hewitt. "We want to accommodate high performers who need alternatives. But you're not seeing any strong words saying we want to encourage people to work part-

---

JOB-SHARING: A GLASS CEILING?

In the 1989 study dealing with corporate flexibility, the consulting firm Catalyst found part-timers earning anywhere from $14,000 to $60,000 a year. But they didn't find any job-sharers earning more than $35,000 a year, suggesting that middle management is the glass ceiling for job-sharers at most companies. Nor did they find a single professional firm—accounting, law, or consulting—that offered job-sharing as an option. While 38 percent of the part-timers in Catalyst's survey had supervisory responsibilities, none of the job-sharers were in supervisory roles.

time. Because we don't." Like lawyers and accountants, consultants are in the service business and the underlying concern is that flexibility will compromise service.

In truth, major law firms, accounting firms, and consulting firms are not by their nature designed for people who need to work less. Regardless of how flexible the policies are, the environment itself breeds workaholism. Client service means being available for a client around the clock. At these high-powered firms, getting ahead still means weekends at the office, 7 A.M. meetings, and midnight rides to the Purolator pickup. In truth, in most corporations and large professional firms, the concept of a reduced schedule remains completely out of sync with prevailing work styles.

If attitude is everything, then attitudes about "power hours" and success may be the greatest single barrier to women's achieving equality in the workplace. If success means a seventy- or eighty-hour work week, it's difficult to imagine many parents who can sustain that level of commitment *over the course of a career* without an extraordinary support system at home.

The barriers to promoting women can be very subtle: they are related to hidden elements of the evaluation process and to unspoken rules about issues like relocation. Flexibility is beginning to creep into the American workplace. But what hasn't changed, even in the most progressive firms, is the fact that a willingness to relocate, to travel, and to spend long hours at the office is still the surest route to promotion. Changing attitudes involves far more than introducing flexible jobs or offering child-care assistance. "This is a very complex and long process," one human resources manager told us. "It will probably take ten or fifteen years. And things won't really change until a new generation moves into management."

THE BOTTOM LINE FOR WOMEN: FLEXIBILITY AND EQUALITY

Equal pay for equal work is still the number one women's issue. Polls tell us it outranks day care, maternity leave, and job discrimination as a subject that concerns women. Rhetoric tells us that, if women give up their spots on the fast track, they will fall behind in their bid for equality. But reality tells us that, for many working parents, particularly parents of young children, a fast-track job *doesn't work,* at least not in 1990, without the support services in place.

As a result, many of the parents we spoke with—while unwilling to stand still—are more than willing to linger for a time below the top echelon in order to have time at home. For these men and women, the prospect of losing their spot on the fast track is a nonissue. They know all too well that the CEO who works eighty hours a week is, by the weight of sheer arithmetic, going to sacrifice time at home. That's a matter of personal choice.

The real problem is this: if women are concentrated in a substratum of part-time and temporary jobs, they will remain second-class employees. If women hop on a slow track, and men stay on the fast track, inequities will result. Or rather, inequities will continue. In 1990, women who work full-time earn, on average, two-thirds of what their male counterparts earn. Women are still concentrated in certain occupations— teachers, secretaries, librarians. They are still not reaching the top of their professions, despite the dramatic rise of women in the work force. Some of the lag relates to discrimination, attitudes that play a role in everything from job evaluations to the support of mentors. The lag also relates to the fact that women have only recently begun their push for equality. They are relatively new to the game.

But the pace at which women have progressed is in part due to the fact that women *do* make career sacrifices for their families—and they are penalized for it. The Catch-22 of flexibility is this: women need it, but, right now at least, flexibility will slow them down professionally. If they cut back their hours, women are perceived as less committed. If they take time off, they may suffer career setbacks.

Discrimination against people holding flexible jobs can range from the obvious to the subtle. Consider this example: Jane Parker has ten years' experience and heads a department with the federal government. She works a four-day week. One of her colleagues works half-time. Not long ago, the entire department was considered for attending a national conference that, according to Jane, is a major annual event. "Not going means being out of touch with what's going on in the field," she says. However, this year, because of budget cuts, not everyone could go. Who was cut from the conference rolls? The two professionals who work shorter hours. Parker was visibly upset. "That's the first time anything like this has happened to me. It's obvious that they had to base the cut on something. They based it on the number of hours a week we spend at the office."

Marcia Thurgood found herself in a similar situation. She had worked in the communications department of a New York financial company for three years, two of those on an abbreviated schedule. Despite her part-time status, she had earned a promotion and, at one point, supervised seven people on a thirty-hour a week schedule. But when higher-ups decided to reorganize the department, she was—literally—the last person in the department to know. Her boss informed her that her new role would be a secure one. "I could work as many hours as I wanted, he said, when he told me my new title," she says. "Somehow, by working less I had sent a message to management: as long as I have a part-time job, I don't care what my title is, what I do, or whether I move up," says Marcia. The assumption was: part-timers are not interested in their career development. Displeased with the offer, as well as the treatment, she ended up leaving the company.

Thurgood and Parker are among lucky part-timers who enjoy the status of management-level titles, competitive salaries, full benefits, and job security. They're way ahead of the millions of part-time people who have none of those advantages. Or the thousands of contract workers—people who work from home on a regular basis, churning out special projects, writing assignments, and spreadsheets. Eager to negotiate some measure of flexibility, they give up benefits, Social Security, employment security, and all the advantages of traditional employment in the name of flexibility. Just for the record, anyone who does the same job from home as he or she did from an office on a full-time basis *must* be considered a regular employee, by law.

The IRS is beginning to crack down on these contract arrangements, many of which are illegal.

Things are definitely improving. The Catalyst study, which surveyed flexible job-holders at the management and professional levels, shattered some of the prevailing myths surrounding part-timers.

❑ They found that 38 percent of the part-time people interviewed had supervisory responsibilities.

❑ They found part-time salaries at corporations as high as $60,000 a year.

❑ Among professionals, salaries for people on reduced schedules exceeded $100,000 a year. And two-thirds of the accountants and lawyers earned $80,000 or more.

The AWSCPA study cited earlier challenged another myth: AWSCPA found that *women do not necessarily experience career sacrifices when they scale back.* Job-sharers and part-timers can and do get promoted. Not all people on alternative schedules are standing still. These are all positive signs.

What we don't know is whether more flexibility will mean genuine setbacks for women. Here, again, are what seem to be the most critical issues.

❑ How can we fashion more equitable pay and benefit schedules for people who aren't willing to work ten hours a day, or even eight hours a day?

❑ How can we change the way we evaluate work so that it has more to do with what we produce and less to do with hours spent in the office?

❑ How can we change attitudes so that valuable part-time people are perceived as serious, committed, motivated employees with career goals and promotion potential?

The issue of how to create a family-responsive working environment is not one that will be resolved in a decade. But the ten years ahead will be critical in determining what direction we take as a society. The nineties—already dubbed the decade of traditionalism—could potentially wreak havoc on the gains women have made in the workplace.

Here's how Fran Rodgers, president of Work/Family Directions, sees the 1990s: "In the seventies, we focused on the basic issue of the entry of women into the labor force and women themselves focused on preparing for careers in fields that men have traditionally dominated. In the eighties working families and women in particular were good girl scouts. They simply worked hard and did what they were supposed to do. In the nineties, we're finding that not enough has changed to support them and they're getting discouraged. This will be the decade when institutions respond. If that doesn't happen, this will be the decade of women changing their expectations, which is a very troubling, but a very real possibility."

Arlene Johnson of the Conference Board's Work and Family Center echoes those sentiments: "For twenty years, women have been trying to get corporate attention to certain issues, to say, 'I'm here, I'm talented. Let's do something that will make it possible for me to be more productive'. Now, just as employers are starting to see it, women are beginning to say, 'Hey, who needs this?' So the question becomes, will women's ambitions fall off? If that happens, then the movitation for a lot of change that's occurring will fall off as well."

To kick off the new decade, *Newsweek* magazine published a special edition on the American family. In it, they published the results of yet another poll. More than two-thirds (68 percent) of those polled agreed that it was important for a family to "make some financial sacrifices so that one parent can stay home to raise the children." If push comes to shove, there's little doubt which parent these people have in mind. Herein lies the rub:

❑ Women want to work. In a 1989 *Time*/CNN poll conducted by Yankelovitch, when women were asked, "Do you think that you would keep your job even if you did not need the income your job provides?" two-thirds (67 percent) of working women said yes. That, despite the fact that among all women surveyed,

82 percent felt it was either somewhat or very difficult to "have it all"—to be married, have children, and have a successful career.

❏ Many women must work. According to the Women's Bureau of the Department of Labor, 58 percent of working women are either divorced, widowed, never married, or married to someone who earns less than $15,000 a year.

❏ Women have demonstrated that they're more than willing to give up time with their families to achieve success in their jobs, if that's what it takes. They have been more than willing to pay the price of equality.

❏ Women like to work. They seem to derive a great deal of satisfaction from it. Study after study—cited in sources ranging from *Working Woman* magazine to the *Des Moines Register*—report that women experience high levels of job satisfaction, oftentimes higher levels than among men.

❏ Finally, women are doing just as good a job as men—although they still make less money and find themselves in lower positions. The problem for women is that they are still expected to do two full-time jobs. Given that fact, for vast numbers of women the work/family dilemma becomes the central issue of their lives.

PART
II

HOW TO GET THE FLEXIBLE JOB YOU WANT

6

MAKING THE FLEXIBLE CHOICE

Who wants flexibility?

Judy Nealon. She slips out of bed on Sunday mornings at 6 A.M., tiptoes into her living room with a steaming cup of coffee and the newspaper. Ahh! Peace and quiet. When she's lucky, her three children sleep till seven and she has an hour to herself. The rest of the week her full-time job as human resources vice-president for an international management consulting company keeps her running at full tilt. She is tired of "practicing time management twenty-four hours a day." A four-day work week would suit her fine.

George Kraus. After fifteen years as a computer analyst, the daily grind of commuting an hour each way and working in an orange cubicle has gotten him down. Besides, his kids are growing up and he hasn't seen enough of them. He'd like to work at home—telecommute.

Jan Simmons. After eight years as the host of her own morning talk show in Baton Rouge, she took time off to be with her three sons. She misses the glamour of television news.

Now that the boys are growing up, she'd like to get back into the business. But not full-time.

These parents like work. They also like their families. They want to balance both. They want a way to work that makes economic sense, provides some sense of fulfillment, and still leaves time for the people they love. They want flexibility.

You may think it incongruous that an idea direct from the corporate boardroom could help you discover a way to work less. But Michael Kipp, strategic planner for the American Management Association, says the basics of the corporate planning process can help anybody at a crossroads.

According to Kipp, plotting the future of a Fortune 500 company or your own career should have similar beginnings. There are three questions to ask at the outset:

❏ Where are you now?

❏ Where do you want to go?

❏ How are you going to get there?

Simple questions? Sure. Easy to answer? Not usually.

Try them on yourself. Many parents have already figured that more flexibility at work would simplify their lives at home. But they don't know how to turn the concept into reality. In this chapter and the next, we will guide you down the path toward flexibility.

Commitments made are sometimes difficult to keep. In an era when the mortgage can eat up more than half the monthly income, even women committed to full-time motherhood are finding they simply can't afford it. Consider the fact that only 7 percent of U.S. households operate like Terri Mitchell's. When her oldest son was born seven years ago, Terri left a communications management job to stay home with her baby. Her husband, Joe, worked long hours launching a construction business. "I have said ever since I made the decision to stay home with Michael, that as long as my children are here, I won't go back to work unless I have to," she relates. "Well, now I have to."

Back when Joe started his business, home building was a growth industry. Now, with real estate in a slump, times are tough. Last year they worked through their meager savings; Joe is interviewing for full-time management positions and the couple may have to consider relocation. Not incidentally, they are also expecting their third child. Says Terri: "I lie awake at night asking myself, Where will this baby be born? How will we pay the bills?"

As Terri sees it, the obvious solution is for her to go back to work. "But," she says, "I just can't face the thought of returning full-time, not with two young boys and an infant at home. I just couldn't do it."

So Terri approached her former employer about a flexible job. Because she had kept in touch with her former supervisor and had occasionally done project work, the door was open. They knew she was reliable. They agreed to discuss a flexible arrangement.

While returning to work part-time can ease financial strain and definitely provide a better balance, the transition from home to work is often fraught with tension. Women heading into the work force after months or years at home full-time express apprehension about everything from a fear of technology, to sagging skill levels, to the prospect of pulling together an appropriate working wardrobe. They worry a lot about the cost and availability of quality child care and wonder how they will restore their professional confidence levels to previous highs.

Said one former stockbroker and full-time mother considering a shortened schedule: "I don't even remember how the business world talks anymore. While I've been home with my kids, I haven't read the business pages. I've been lucky to read anything."

Recently while I, Lynn, was picking up my son at preschool, another mother with two young children in tow approached me to ask about my flexible job.

"I would give anything to have a job like yours," proclaimed Cindy Hazelton, after hearing about my arrangement. A former budget analyst with an MBA from a midwestern university, at one time Hazelton had been on the financial services fast track. But after the birth of her second child, she decided motherhood required more of her attention. "I'd love to get back into it, but I can't imagine that anyone would hire me. I'm never sure of my schedule. Often, I'd have to go in late and leave early."

It's not likely that anyone would hire Hazelton if she could not commit to *some* kind of regular schedule. Once she decides how much time she *is* willing to devote to work, a flexible job is her best option. And it would provide her employer with a competent staff member.

There are too few examples of women able to reenter the work force with the flexibility they'd prefer. They've been forced to choose between all or nothing. So, many talented women, like Hazelton, have abandoned their careers rather than spend forty hours a week away from their children. But as the labor pool evaporates, will more flexible opportunities surface?

"Absolutely," says Dan Paperman, human resources senior vice-president for a national health-care company. "Employers won't have a choice. They will consider themselves fortunate to hire someone with a track record. And if training is needed to update their skills, the employer will happily provide it."

The health-care industry's efforts to attract experienced nurses provides a colorful preview of what can happen when available talent is in short supply. Hospitals now offer beefed-up benefits packages, four-day work weeks, and cash incentives to get the best people. Want to work weekends? Take on two twelve-hour nursing shifts and a full week's salary and benefits are yours.

As other industries come up against similar employment challenges, experts say the doors will open more widely for flexibility. That means more women like Hazelton will have a chance to make a professional contribution on terms they can live with.

MAKING THE DECISION TO SCALE BACK ON WORK HOURS

Many parents begin the search for more flexibility from the exhaustion point of a sixty-hour work week. Turning the corner toward a more flexible career can take courage. You've spent years (not to mention dollars) on a top-flight education. Add on several more years for training and hands-on experience in your field. And now, perhaps, just as you've reached your professional stride, you find yourself asking: Should I work less so I can be at home more?

For a successful woman, the decision can take on added meaning. After all, she is viewed as a role model, a mentor, for those on the way up. "I was so afraid of disappointing all the young women in my agency," remembers Ellen Malloy, mother of a two-year-old girl, who left her high-profile, high-paying position with an international ad agency for the chance to spend more time with her daughter. She'd been considered a prime candidate for her division's top job of general manager. Instead she took a three-day-a-week post managing special projects from home. Other women had sought her advice on how to climb the corporate ladder without giving up weekends, friends, and family. After all, few senior women in the organization were married. Even fewer had children. When the announcement came of her new role with the company, she was sure her colleagues would be disappointed. "Instead, I received countless notes and phone calls from people who said they admired what I had done. And they wished they could do it too."

But regardless of your status in the organization, it can still be an agonizing decision. Recalls Susan Elwood, a twenty-nine-year-old new mother and systems analyst who cut back to a three-day work week, "I spent weeks and then months weighing my options. I made lists of pros and cons. I bored all of my friends talking about my dilemma. Some days it seemed that asking for a part-time position was the right thing to do. Other days it seemed preposterous—I had invested so much. Finally one day I just said to myself, Go for it."

Barring a crisis, it takes not only courage, but considerable thought and planning to determine whether a flexible job is right for you. Flexibility can mean cutting out minutes, hours, or days from your work schedule to achieve a better balance. It is an emotional as well as a professional decision. Your child-care situation, finances, career path, lifestyle, and personal priorities all play a role in the decision.

For most people, work is an integral part of their identity. That makes the conflict particularly intense. Previously unwilling or unable to scale back their careers, many parents we talked with were balancing too much. They had reached the breaking point. "I just never had enough time," said one mother. "I wasn't doing anything well and was constantly exhausted from the attempt," commented another. "My work was really suffering because I could not get my daughter out of my mind," said a third. "I wasn't worth much to my company as a full-time employee."

"It was the dinner hour that drove me to a change," recalls Sally Evans, a Des Moines graphic designer. "One evening after work I strode into the kitchen balancing grocery bags and babies, and was struggling to answer the phone. One bag broke open, spilling spaghetti all over the floor. It was forty square feet of pickup sticks! Somehow that was a turning point. I thought to myself, I cannot cope with this any more."

The next evening she sat down with her husband and reviewed their financial picture. They determined that by eliminating the cost of child care two days a week and cutting back their travel and entertainment expenses, they could live comfortably on three-fifths of Sally's earnings, combined with Bob's full-time income. Hopefully, she would be able to convince her employer that the plan was workable.

For me, Lynn, and for many of the people we interviewed, reaching the conclusion that a more flexible work arrangement could restore some order to our harried lives did not come easily. It was often a lengthy and sometimes painful process.

As the vice-president for international marketing for Quality International, my job often took me to places like Paris, Milan, Mexico City, and Berlin. At a different time in my life it would have been the dream job—a professional challenge and a chance to make a difference in my company, not to mention the travel itself. But as the mother of two small children, I was in the right place at the wrong time. Each time I pulled my passport out of the drawer I was forced to reexamine my priorities.

One Friday evening in April of 1988, I found myself in a

hotel room overlooking Sydney Harbor, with the instantly recognizable Opera House as the backdrop. I was tired after a long day of meetings but was determined to take in a bit of the city before leaving the next day. I ordered one ticket (which was depressing enough) for an evening performance at the Opera House. As curtain time approached I walked across the plaza, stopping to watch the birds dive for fish among the boats anchored for the night. A heavy mist was falling, which probably served to further dampen my mood. Leaning on the railing, watching the water, I couldn't help but wonder, Just what am I doing here? I am halfway around the world, alone, away from my husband and two sons.

As I walked on toward the Opera House I found myself in the midst of happy couples outfitted in evening dress, obviously planning to attend the opening of the ballet season, which I knew was scheduled for this evening.

Once in my seat, I didn't pay much attention to the performance. I spent most of the evening engulfed in my own personal drama. What could I do next? How could I change my life? And for me—a radical thought—how could I scale back my job?

Before I left Australia I bought a painting titled "Sydney at Night." Each time I look at it hanging in my dining room, I am reminded of the night my life changed.

As it was for so many people I interviewed, and will perhaps be for you, the process of separating my personal self from my professional being was intense. I had become so wrapped up in my career, it was if I had to peel off one layer at a time until I reached the part of me that was first a mother and a wife. It was only then that I could assess my options realistically.

I considered everything from bidding our nanny farewell and staying home full-time to finding a part-time job that required less mental and physical energy. I was mindful, too, of the effect that eliminating my salary would have on our lifestyle. And I couldn't help but wonder how my ego would hold up once I actually relinquished my senior management position. There was one thing of which I became certain. There had to be a meaningful place for me somewhere between "Super-woman" and "housewife." And if there wasn't, I would have to create one.

Four months went by before the solution became evident and Susan and I proposed our job-sharing arrangement.

FACING REALITY

Before you propose a flexible job to your employer or leave the security of your firm in search of flexibility, think carefully about the realities of working less and *your* reasons for wanting a change.

No work arrangement, however flexible, will relieve all the pressures of mixing a career with parenthood. As Marcia Klein-man of Options, a Philadelphia-based human resources consult-ing firm, points out, "In planning for a new job you must be realistic in your expectations. You can't expect to have *everything* you want on your terms."

Consider the following issues:

❑ *What's wrong with this picture?* Just what is it about your current job that doesn't suit you? Is it too stressful? Is your commute too long? Are the hours too many? Are you required to travel? Is your boss unsympathetic to the demands of your family? Will flexibility make a difference?

One woman we spoke with in Phoenix said she had considered asking to turn her full-time job as an insurance adjuster into a part-time position, even though her family needed her full-time salary and benefits. After giving it consid-erable thought, she realized it wasn't the hours she didn't like, it was the job. She changed industries instead of her hours and income.

❑ *Are you a flexible person?* Many flexible jobs require that the incumbent be flexible too. In some cases, by virtue of your hours alone, you'll be out of sync with the traditional work force. Will you feel comfortable leaving early while others are still concentrating on the day's tasks, or coming in at midday when the office is already in full swing?

Some bosses, like this one in Washington, D.C., will expect a payback in your own flexible currency. "When my employer offered me flexibility, he expected the same in return," commented technical writer Susan Lang, whose work arrangement allows her to pick her children up after school.

"His expectation was that I would be more willing to take on projects at the last minute or change gears in midstream. Sometimes this was a little unsettling, but I felt it was part of the deal so I went along with it."

❑ *Can your ego take it?* If yours is a fragile ego, beware the loss of status that sometimes accompanies a reduction in hours. How will you feel when the big meeting takes place on your day off or someone refers to you as "just a part-timer"?

"I still remember the day one of my subordinates went to a colleague to solve a major problem that cropped up on my day off," recounts Andrea Stillman. "When I asked him why he didn't call for my advice, he said he didn't want to bother me and it needed on-the-spot resolution. I knew this was inevitable, but it made me feel so unimportant."

❑ *Can your bank account take it?* Not everyone can afford to work less. For some, the romantic notion of sunny afternoons at the playground or field trips with the second-graders obscures the harsh realities of balancing the family budget. A reduced schedule usually means reduced income. So before you set forth any proposal, carefully review the ramifications a change in workstyle will have on your lifestyle.

"We used to be able to take the kids out for dinner now and then," reports Chicagoan Patty Skinner, who recently scaled back her $30,000 nursing job to half-time. "Now we tell them we're eating at the Skinner Inn. That's right here and that's what we can afford. Last week," she adds "someone asked us to go to the circus. I felt bad saying no but circus tickets are no longer in our budget."

❑ *Is your child-care arrangement flexible?* How will a shortened schedule affect your child-care arrangements? Will your day-care center or provider accept your new arrangement? Will you have the flexibility to alternate hours or days if your new position requires it? According to Catalyst researcher Christine Scordato, participants in their study on flexible jobs reported that although flexibility at work meant more time available for families, it did not translate into lower child-care costs for two reasons. First, part-time child care was not available in their communities; and, second, a full-time care arrangement provided the flexibility to work extra hours when necessary. But creative solutions do exist. Two nurses at Children's Hospital in Washington, D.C., were able to split a job and a babysitter, each working two and a half days. A job-sharing pair at Michigan manufacturer Steelcase actually found each other through the in-home provider they both rely on.

Most family day-care and in-home providers welcome children on a part-time schedule, but centers seem less flexible. "If we take one child on Monday, Wednesday, and Friday," explains the director of an Ohio day-care center, "we have to match them, for staffing purposes, with another child who wants to come Tuesday and Thursday. It is more costly and time-consuming for us to have to do that."

Added another day-care staffer in explaining their "only full-timers welcome" policy, "It's hard for the little ones to fit in if they only come a few days a week."

❑ *Are you a good communicator?* Job-sharing, for example, will require that you sharpen your interpersonal and communication skills. Many flexible jobs require more than average amounts of communication with management and co-workers to keep things running smoothly.

You must also be resourceful. For example, on a four-day work schedule, one manager delivers her staff instructions for day five by early-morning fax. She receives an end-of-the-day wrap-up the same way. Two job-sharers in Michigan found communications improved when they targeted their at-home phone calls for the children's nap time.

❏ *Does a lateral career move or a step down fit into your long-term goals?* If you've always imagined yourself in the corner office, opting for more flexibility doesn't mean you won't get there. Some, however, would argue that jumping off the fast track will slow you down. Are you prepared to take that risk?

THE SEARCH BEGINS

When Bostonian Anita Black decided to look for "the highest-level flexible job" she could find, she fell back on all the advice she had given to students who sought her guidance as a university placement director.

Scour the professional journals, tell everyone you know about your job search, read the want ads, talk to people who have jobs like the one you want, she had told them. Set goals and follow up. The problem Anita encountered now was that she didn't know anyone who had the kind of job she wanted.

She tried answering newspaper ads for full-time jobs by sending her résumé and a letter explaining what she had in mind. She got no response. "I had written what I thought was a very impressive letter. I explained that I was a hard worker and that I could do as much work as most people in half the time. In retrospect I realize that was the wrong approach. I'm sure they read it, rolled their eyes, and tossed it in the trash."

Next she tried networking. "I identified five people who knew me professionally and invited them to lunch one by one. Four of the five were women. I told each of them what I was looking for. They were all very pleasant, and offered me personal encouragement. They wished me luck but I could tell they were a little skeptical."

A few weeks later, however, one offered her a job. She accepted.

Anita was lucky. After all, she was an experienced placement counselor. What better starting point for any job search? Typically, looking for a flexible job is more difficult than beginning a traditional job search. Nevertheless, many of the same rules apply. Explains Linda Marks, a California career development specialist who speaks frequently on how to find a flexible job, "It is not easy to find a less-than-full-time job. You must be very creative, use all your resources."

WHO CAN HELP IN YOUR SEARCH FOR A FLEXIBLE JOB?

When I, Lynn, graduated from Arizona State University, I began my first professional job search. Living a few thousand miles from where I had grown up, I quickly realized how much I had previously counted on the "hometown advantage." Employment opportunities came from friends of my parents, teacher referrals, or even neighbors.

Now, with few contacts in the Phoenix area, I was forced to rely on the university career-placement service—which rarely listed jobs in my field of journalism—or, worse, on the classifieds.

I learned swiftly about "the hidden job market," that bastion of opportunity that lies just *inside* the door of almost every organization. So how does one go about uncovering opportunity—particularly flexible opportunity?

After studying the mating dance of employers and seekers of flexible jobs for nearly two years, we have combed out the four best bets for flexible employment opportunity.

It typically happens like this:

❏ You want flexibility and your current employer doesn't want to lose you, so you stay—three days a week (they've invested in you).

❏ Or, your mother's best friend is vice-president of human resources for Company X and she would be willing to give you a shot at proving yourself four days a week (in other words, you know somebody).

❑ Or, you are a very competent tax attorney and the law firm of Smith, Smith & Jones needs a competent tax attorney tomorrow. Will they take you tomorrow—thirty hours a week? You bet! (You've got what they want!).

❑ Or, Best Company, Inc., has a flexible jobs policy that has the competition green with envy. Why? Because the best employees around, like you, are flooding the gates looking for flexible jobs now or reserving their place for the future.

You get the idea. Here's more:

❑ *Your current employer may be your best bet!* Throughout our conversations with more than a hundred men and women in flexible jobs and our review of the most recent surveys, one fact was clear: flexibility goes first to those already on the payroll. The choice flexible assignments are negotiated by valued employees within their own organizations. In the next chapter, we discuss at length negotiating with your supervisor for a flexible arrangement.

❑ *Someone in there knows you.* Label it what you like: the old boys' network, friends of the family, old friends from school, golf buddies, sorority sisters, fraternity brothers, or fellow churchgoers. It is, as they say, not always what you know but whom you know.

Hiring a known commodity ups the comfort factor for most managers. "Employers hire people they know, people they like. It's an insurance policy," explains Judy Nelson, vice-president for human resources for Best Western International. "And if I don't know the candidate, but someone I respect provides a recommendation, that's the next best thing."

You may begin by interviewing for a full-time position. But knowing you have a personal "in" will give you confidence to negotiate the scheduling terms you want.

This point argues for telling your family, friends, and neighbors about your search for a flexible alternative. Ann Heldenberg quit her high-pressure financial services position to head up the accounting department at her husband's manufacturing business three days a week. Ann explains: "He'd been looking for someone, but didn't even think to talk to me until he heard me discussing an accounting job with someone else."

Don't overlook this resource: *former employers*. If your old boss can't help you now, perhaps he or she knows someone who can. Assuming you left on good terms, he or she may be able to point you in the right direction. When urban housing specialist Carolyn McMillan's old supervisor heard through the grapevine that she was back in the market for a flexible post, he called her and offered her a three-day-a-week job.

❑ *Your skills are in demand.* As the labor market tightens, it will be a seller's market for those with sought-after skills. Today, for example, nurses and computer programmers with good credentials have little difficulty working as much or as little as they like.

Smaller companies, too, often need senior level talent but can't afford the full-time price tag. George Atkins runs a small market research firm in a suburb of Washington, D.C. He recently hired a senior researcher for half the salary he paid her full-time predecessor. The new employee works half days.

"I need the upscale talent, someone with experience and expertise in the field," explains Atkins. "But with the ebb and flow of our work, it helps my bottom line to pay for the minimum number of hours. I add to the payroll if our work load can justify it."

❑ *Flexibility is the trend.* The Association of Part-Time Professionals (APTP), based in Falls Church, Virginia (see Part III: Resources), provides monthly listings of management and professional flexible jobs for members. While APTA addresses national issues, at this writing most of its workshops and job listings are relevant primarily for Washington, D.C., and its suburbs. However, the number of its national leads are increasing. Meanwhile, local chapters have opened in Boston and Hampton, New Hampshire; others in California, New York, and Texas are in the formative stages.

APTP recommends that you check in with your professional associations and journals for job-bank listings of flexible positions or full-time postings that could be negotiated to fit your lifestyle. The Women's Bar Association of Washington, D.C., for example, runs a part-time employment exchange bank. The Public Relations Society of America (PRSA) also lists flexible job opportunities in its newsletter.

Don't overlook the business or lifestyle sections of your local newspaper for stories about start-up companies or organizations that might have a need for your special skills.

As interest in flexible work arrangements heightens, placement services have cropped up to serve specific strands of the professional market. Legal placement agencies have opened their doors in major cities across the country, matching lawyers who voluntarily left the fast track with clients who need top-notch professional services.

Alternatrack (see Part III: Resources) was started by two former Wall Street women in New York who got tired of "going to work in the dark and coming home in the dark." The placement company provides flexible opportunities for experienced professionals in law or financial services. Co-owners Suzanne Renfrit Moore and Karen Cook hook up candidates with companies large and small who need such services on a less-than-full-time basis. Alternatrack is also experimenting with the creation of job-sharing pairs to fill full-time slots. At this writing, applicants far outweigh available jobs (600 to five). But Renfrit Moore and Cook say they are working with many companies to open up more slots for their clients.

Even though most organizations with flexible job policies require an in-house track record before a flexible schedule is approved, that is subject to change. "Just because it has never happened before doesn't mean it won't happen tomorrow," said Deborah Hall, a spokesperson for Michigan-based Steelcase. "That's how things have changed around here in the past. Our boss has just said, 'Let's try it and see if it works.' "

If you're looking for flexibility, try your local government office. Since 1978, the federal government has been encouraged to expand flextime, job-sharing, and part-time professional work opportunities for government employees. More than

50,000 permanent government workers currently share jobs or work shortened hours. While these positions require supervisory approval, the government does not require full-time service before a flexible job can be filled.

Some state and local governments have flexible job policies and hire from the outside. For example, New York State runs a flexible job bank. The city of Milwaukee offers job-sharing and four-day work weeks to its employees.

While the best jobs don't always make it to the newspaper, lots of good ones do. Scan the classified columns for flexible opportunities or for positions posted with companies recognized for their work/family policies.

Once you've made the choice to pursue the flexible options, you know where you are going. In the next chapter, we'll show you how to get there through effective negotiation.

7

THE NEGOTIATING
TABLE

At age forty, Sandy Bevins was in an enviable position. A CPA at a large public accounting firm in Tucson, she had management responsibilities and was on a steady track of salary increases and promotions. She had a delightful four-year-old daughter. She was making more money than she ever imagined she might; she worked longer hours too. And now that she "had it all," Bevins was thinking about ditching the whole professional picture unless she could negotiate some flexibility. She wanted more time for family and friends.

There was a complicating factor. Two other CPAs in the firm had negotiated flexible arrangements after the birth of their children. Six months after they returned to the office, both women quit. Would the partners sanction yet another flexible arrangement? It was as if she began the negotiating process with two strikes against her. Bevins carefully assembled a plan, outlining how she could meet the firm's objectives without sacrificing too much of her personal life. Her own past performance and commitment to the firm won management's confidence; they all agreed upon a thirty-hour work week.

Walking into your employer's office to negotiate for a flexible job can be a mystifying proposition—if you are not prepared. In this chapter we will provide step-by-step guidelines for assessing the dynamics of your situation and specific strategies for successful negotiation.

NEGOTIATING FOR THE JOB YOU NEED AND WANT

A country club membership. A company car. The chance to travel. Those were the items most common to the negotiating table in years past. For today's executive, the priorities are changing. An increasing number of employees—men and women—are trading such tangible rewards of success for more work flexibility.

Still, the professional who so skillfully worked his or her way up the corporate ladder—negotiating raises, deals, and contracts along the way—shudders at the prospect of negotiating for *less*—less time in the office.

"I felt very uncomfortable going into my boss's office to propose a flexible job," commented Arizonan Sarah Gilday, an award-winning advertising executive with two small children. "I just didn't have any idea what he would say. That was scary."

Sarah shouldn't have felt insecure about discussing her future with her supervisor. She had been with the agency for five years. She had proven herself. Her work was well respected by clients, peers, and agency management. Yet because she was going to bring up a "new" idea, one never broached in her workplace before, she was apprehensive.

When two people like Gilday and her boss get together to talk about change—a change in title, salary, responsibility, or the structure of a job—a negotiation is likely to occur. There is no ready-made formula for negotiating flexibility. You must do your own detective work. Then, with information in hand, weave your own successful strategy. The better prepared you are at the outset of the process, the more likely it is you will win points with your logic. After all, the best way to persuade someone is with a strong argument.

Below are basic guidelines for effective negotiation. By working through these four areas you will emerge prepared to begin the negotiating game. *We will discuss each of these efforts in more detail as the chapter progresses.*

❏ *Know your subject:* Determine who it is that will be making the decision about your flexible opportunity. Study that person carefully.

❏ *Define your mutual interests:* Know what's in flexibility for you and what's in it for your employer.

❏ *Be prepared:* Remember the old scouting motto? Do your research and develop a detailed and thorough plan to present to your employer.

❏ *Develop a strategy:* Know how, when, and where you will present the elements of your plan.

Now, to further clarify your goals and to crystallize your negotiating tactics, ask yourself these questions:

1. What do I have to lose by proceeding? Will I pay any personal or professional penalties? Do I risk losing my current job by raising the subject with my boss?
2. Have I identified all the players in this game? Will the answer be forthcoming from my boss? Or will he or she be forced to take the issue to higher ups? Do I know my boss's superiors? Do they know me and my work?
3. Are there time constraints here? Does my personal situation demand an immediate answer? Would it pay to wait? Will my chances of winning flexibility be greater, for example, in the next fiscal year?
4. How and where will I carry out these negotiations?
5. Do I have a fallback position? Am I prepared to compromise if my pitch for the perfect work arrangement is not accepted? Where is the middle ground?
6. If I am forced to remain with the status quo, have I won or lost anything? Am I prepared to accept that as an option?

As you read more about the negotiating process in this chapter, remember, in a successful negotiation everyone wins.

FINDING JOB FLEXIBILITY WITH YOUR CURRENT EMPLOYER

It was her first child. And during the first few weeks of her three-month maternity leave, Nancy Trainer, thirty-four, fell in love with motherhood. It was time, she determined, to pare back her hours as director of an international sales division. Her professional responsibilities included sales and marketing and the management of three other salespeople. There was also considerable travel involved.

Her situation was this: Trainer wanted to work three days a week but retain her manager's role. She knew it would be nearly impossible to maintain both her sales and marketing efforts on a three-day-a-week schedule, and to fit in travel and management responsibilities as well.

Her solution: after studying the individual components of her job, she proposed the allocation of one of her three sales territories to another up-and-coming salesperson. With the savings from her reduced salary she could hire a marketing specialist on a shortened schedule.

Trainer's proposal to her supervisor also highlighted these no-cost benefits to the company:

❑ One individuals's focused efforts on marketing

❑ The opportunity to provide career development for a high-performing salesperson

❑ Continuity with clients and staff

❑ The retention of a senior and valued employee

Not wanting to lose Trainer's contacts and expertise in the industry, her supervisor approved her innovative plan.

According to a 1989 study by Catalyst, the "single greatest motivator for companies to explore the use of flexible work arrangements for management and professional employees is retention of high-performing, valued employees." Of the forty-seven companies they surveyed, 68 percent cited this as their primary motivation for making changes. Another 14 percent pointed to "changing work force demographics," a factor closely allied with retention.

As one senior marketing executive said in approving a job-sharing arrangement, "This is a case of one plus one equals three." He concluded that the pair's combined experience on the job, plus the relationships they had with employees throughout the company, was a commodity that could not easily be replaced. Indeed, in this manager's view, retaining both professionals constituted added value for his company.

If you're good at your job, your supervisor knows it and will want to keep you. Replacing a well-trained employee is a costly, often unpleasant experience that few supervisors welcome. Nevertheless, don't expect management to knock on *your* door with a flexible opportunity. It happens, but not often. If you can envision more flexibility with your present employer, here are steps you can take to improve the changes that your organization will approve your flexible plan.

ASSESSING THE CORPORATE CULTURE

Linking work and family in a discussion about the workplace is relatively new. We have traditionally been encouraged to consider these two aspects of our lives as independent entities. Employees have been urged to avoid even the potential for overlap. Says Fran Rodgers of Work/Family Directions: "Women still think family is a dirty secret at work."

"If you want to be considered for top management," parents were told, "for heaven's sake, don't talk about your children in the office." A more serious mistake was allowing them to be seen.

Recall the telling scenes from the 1979 movie *Kramer vs. Kramer*. The beleaguered single dad, played by Dustin Hoffman, struggled to be a good, caring father while holding down a demanding job in advertising. We cringed as he sprinted from important client meetings to his son's school activities. The pain of it all was evident on his face. The stress and strain came through in his voice. His attempts to relax with his son in the evenings, to find that quality time somewhere between bath and bed, are familiar scenes to many of us.

Ted Kramer's employers had little sympathy for this character trying so desperately to balance it all. It was clear that their agenda wasn't his. In their view, Kramer's head and heart were in the wrong place.

But changes in the way we live since the time of Ted Kramer's story have put these two parts of life on a collision course, and business is being forced to deal with the merger. In recent years, companies *have* become more responsive to the needs of working parents. Experts agree that most employers will become more flexible as demographics change the consistency of the labor pool.

Meanwhile, it is not enough for a company's *senior* management to embrace a human resource proposal. If the employee is to reap the day-to-day benefits of these policy changes, each manager and supervisor down the line must be trained to accept and effectively implement flexible arrangements.

As you assess your corporate culture—the style in which things happen day to day—look not only to existing clues but to a bit of history.

Taking in the Track Record. If your company has a good track record for supporting and promoting women professionally, chances are the issue of providing job flexibility has at least been discussed. However, that doesn't mean you will know about it. The movement in most organizations can be characterized as slow and silent.

Fewer than 40 percent of the companies participating in the Catalyst study on flexible jobs, for example, reported the existence of a formal policy governing flexible arrangements, even though the jobs were there. These flexible arrangements are often negotiated *ad hoc* and are largely unaccounted for on human resources department rosters.

Is the Company Innovative at Heart? Often the decision to move ahead on work/family issues is made in the same way other innovations have evolved in the workplace. Does your organization encourage the free flow of opinions and ideas? Is management prone to formal written policies? Or does change happen informally? Historically, has innovation been a cornerstone of your company's overall style?

At Apple Computers, a company known for its state-of-the-art computer technology, human resources vice-president Deborah Biondolillo says that, despite intense competitive pressures in their industry, decisions within her organization are made "as much on an intuitive basis as an analytical basis." In 1988 Apple opened an on-site child-care facility, staffed by experienced and well-paid providers. Had the decision to create the center for their employees been based on financial data, "I don't think we could have sold it," explains Deborah. "I think there is a very strong belief in this company that the environment you create for your employees may cost you a little more, but it pays off in the kind of people you attract and in their productivity."

Work- and Family-Friendly. You probably have a sense as to whether your company has warmed to the concept of flexible jobs. Its willingness to address other work/family issues is usually a good indication of the corporate appetite for flexibility. Have child-care, parental leave, or eldercare programs been introduced? Given the broad scope of these issues, some companies choose to focus their initial policy-development efforts on a single component. Meanwhile, they may be open to other family supportive programs like flexible jobs.

Most important, find out if there are other employees with flexible arrangements. If so, the ice has been broken.

If your organization is even marginally supportive of flexibility, your negotiating prospects are that much stronger. If there are no positive signs, remember that in every organization, someone has been first.

WHO DECIDES?

Janet Stephens had devoted nearly her entire professional career—almost nine years—to the communications department of a large Pennsylvania-based manufacturing company. She and her husband had decided early in her pregnancy that putting their new baby in day care was something they didn't want to do. So Stephens informed her boss she would not be returning. She even began helping him find her replacement.

It quickly became clear that replacing someone with Stephens's considerable talent, experience, and contacts would not be easy or inexpensive. Richard Tompkins, her supervisor, suggested she consider telecommuting—move the computer home, hook up to the office via modem, and continue her career from a spare bedroom.

"Ours is a very conservative company. I never thought they would let me do it," recalls Stephens. "No one had ever done anything like that before."

Even though Stephens's boss was all for the idea, the decision went all the way to the CEO's office for final approval. This top-level involvement is a reflection of the conservative culture of the organization. At the same time, it is an example of a company creating new rules for an employee they believed was too valuable to lose.

"There will always be the individuals who can get their act together and make a good argument—be persuasive and good enough as individuals that they will convince a company," says Arlene Johnson of the Conference Board. "They will find a sympathetic, understanding, or flexible person to go along with their plan. Someone who is an innovator at heart."

Most often, that person is the employee's immediate supervisor. He or she interprets the company policy, if there is one. Or the supervisor "creates" an informal company response, often on his or her own, to an employee request for flexibility.

So, even if your company has a management-approved flexible jobs policy, it's likely that your supervisor will determine if and to what extent flexibility is allowed.

Indeed, the role of the supervisor as power broker becomes significant. A recent study of working mothers conducted by the National Council of Jewish Women reported that "trying to juggle the demands of job and family" was highly stressful—no surprise to those doing it. The study found that strong support from husbands *and immediate supervisors* could significantly reduce stress levels for working mothers with young children.

There are companies, like many of those listed in Chapter 4, where flexible jobs are accepted and supervisors are trained to help reduce the kinds of stress that show up in studies like this one. Employees researching flexible options within the best companies can turn to the human resource department *as well as to their supervisors* for counseling, guidance, and encouragement.

For example, in and near Denver, 2,500 U S West Communications employees work from home or alternate sites as part of the company's forward-thinking telecommuting project. Employees interested in telecommuting are provided a two-part checklist intended to help supervisors determine the appropriateness of this workstyle for specific jobs. This calls for input from both employee and supervisor. Jointly they clarify how the work arrangement will solve company problems, and they arrive at measurement objectives and time frames.

The employee works on the second section of the checklist to study how his or her job will work in the home environment, and provides details about the proposed workspace, support services or hardware needed, as well as his or her own expectations for the work arrangement. The team of supervisor and employee then decides the arrangement's prospects for success.

Will it be your supervisor who will make the decision, or at least be influential in the final crafting of schedules? If you can be confident on that score, preparing is easier. "After I was sure who it was that would be determing my future," commented Liza Niles, a Chicago-based government attorney who negotiated a four-day work week, "I studied that person carefully for weeks. After a while, I felt I knew him well enough to develop the kind of proposal he would accept."

REDEFINING YOUR JOB

The first step in the negotiating process is knowing what you want. A realistic analysis of your job and your lifestyle will help you design a flexible schedule that works.

With your personal financial situation as your reality backdrop, create the kind of work/family scene that would restore balance to your life. How much time are you prepared to devote to your work? What are your career-versus-family priorities? What aspects of your job do you enjoy most? What responsibilities, if any, are you willing to give up?

It may help to look at the issue from three perspectives. We label them *time, content, and form.*

Time: How much time are you willing to devote to work?

Are you looking for a dramatic shift in focus—significantly less time on the job? Or will just a few hours shaved from your office schedule relieve the pressure? How much time can you afford to cut back?

Content: Will the new position be interesting and challenging? Will the work be meaningful? Will it propel *your* career on an upward path? Will this work be respected by your peers? How important is this issue to you now?

Among the women we interviewed, some, like Bostonian Madeline Dorsey, were prepared for not only fewer hours but less of an intellectual strain. An enthusiastic entrepreneur, Dorsey had worked for seven years to build up her own retail ice cream business in a small resort town. Its peak came simultaneously with news that the adoption of her first child was imminent. Ready for a change in focus, she sold her business. Now she works in an art gallery three days a week. The new position is less demanding and allows her to pursue her keen interest in art history. And, of course, there is more time for family.

Form: You have the ability to shape your new flexible position. Study this mix: the time you've allocated to work, your levels of responsibility, your personal workstyle, and your corporate culture. Given the final formula, which flexible option is likely to suit your needs and your employer's too? Are you a job-sharer? Will shortened hours work for you? Would setting up shop at home make sense? Full-time? A mixed schedule of days?

If you can decide how much *time* you are prepared to work, and the nature of the *job content* you're seeking, that should bring you closer to defining the *form* your flexible position will take. Now an analysis of the specific components of your job should make the picture even more clear.

WORK UNITS

You can determine if your current job will fit into the ideal you have created by dividing it into work units. By labeling individual components of your job, you will be able to rank them in order of their importance to you and your supervisor.

You will also be able to add, subtract, or reshape them into a form that will give you the flexibility you need. Your current job description will be useful for this exercise. You will be able to determine which work units

❑ best suit your skills

❑ are most interesting and challenging to you

❑ could be shared with another person

❑ could be delegated to a subordinate

❑ could be accomplished before or after traditional office hours

❑ could be accomplished at home

❑ could be eliminated from the job description

❑ could be reassigned to a colleague

❑ could be reassigned to another department

❑ are a company priority

Ultimately, you will determine which units will comprise your flexible job.

Let's review a simple example.

Melissa Santamour, twenty-nine, writes the company and employee newsletters for a national insurance company. Two months ago she received top ratings and a raise during her second annual review. Now, as her daughter's first birthday approaches, she simply wants to spend more time at home.

Before making any proposals to her supervisor, she reexamined her job in the context of her lifestyle, reviewing the components of time, content, and form. Then she analyzed the job and broke out the individual work units.

Time: Even one extra day at home with no professional interruptions would make a difference. She'd have more time to spend with her child, run errands, and keep personal appointments. Gaining the extra time at home, she determined, was worth giving up some responsibility and income. One less day on the job would logically mean losing one-fifth of her salary. She and her husband felt that was manageable.

Content: Santamour enjoyed the research, interviewing, and writing aspects of her job. She found the production side of newsletter publishing repetitive and less challenging. It was important to her, in terms of future career growth, to continue developing her writing skills.

Form: Briefly, Santamour considered looking for a job-sharing partner. She abandoned the idea early, recognizing her own strong sense of independence. She would prefer working shortened hours or working at home.

Santamour broke her job into these six *work units*: 1) generating story ideas (through informal interviewing and research); 2) interviews and research; 3) writing; 4) editing; 5) production; 6) general administration.

After analyzing the work units of her job, Santamour came to these conclusions:

❏ She wanted to retain the writing and editing functions of her job.

❏ She would be willing to part with the production responsibilities and could foresee them being reassigned. An assistant in the department, who was looking for more responsibility, would welcome the opportunity.

❏ Some of the interviews could be handled by phone from home.

❏ Her personal computer would enable her to complete writing assignments at home.

❏ The remainder of her duties would require her presence in the office.

❏ If the production responsibilities could be reassigned, she felt she could shorten her schedule to three days in the office and one day at home.

Would her company accept her bid for flexibility? Santamour's company had no formal flexible jobs policy. The organization had recently begun holding parenting seminars during the lunch hour and she knew the human resources department was investigating child-care supports for headquarters employees. These were good signs. She also knew that her boss had the support of senior management and her best guess was that it would be his decision. She prepared a formal plan to present to her boss; he liked things in writing. Her recommendations were these:

❑ Santamour could work shortened hours: full days Monday, Wednesday, and Friday in the office and all day Thursday at home. She would save her most difficult writing assignments and some follow-up interviews for Thursday, when she would have the fewest interruptions. She would be off Tuesdays.

❑ Production coordination could be reassigned to the departmental assistant. Santamour would retain all other duties.

❑ Prorating her salary and benefits, she would receive four-fifths of her $28,000 salary, or $22,400.

Her plan was accepted. Here's how you can create a winning plan.

SIX STEPS TOWARD FLEXIBILITY

An essential part of any good negotiation, as previously noted, is careful preparation. Once you have a clear idea of the job you will propose, you are ready for the next step. To ensure that your negotiations for flexibility go smoothly, prepare a complete plan that will *overcome* your company's biases. Include the following six steps:

Step One. Research: Provide information about other people within your organization who have flexible jobs.

❑ Has their experience been successful? If so, why?

❑ If it hasn't worked out, be prepared to explain how you will avoid similar pitfalls.

❑ Provide parallel examples from other companies illustrating successful situations.

❑ Consider providing references (with phone numbers) of managers who have successfully supervised a flexible job.

Step Two. Self-promotion: Remind your supervisor of the good work you have completed for your organization.

❑ Mention past performance reviews, your participation in special projects, awards you have received, and special examples of your particular skill or strengths.

❑ Include congratulatory letters from your file.

❑ In short, provide evidence of your value to the organization.

Step Three. Outline of work: Carefully detail how you see your new position working.

❑ Detail the number of hours you would like to work and when.

❑ Divide your position into units of work, noting which aspects you think are most important.

❑ Also note which units you will handle.

❑ Provide suggestions for splitting the remaining units among other employees or for hiring other, less expensive staff to take on less challenging assignments.

❑ If yours is a management job, outline how you will delegate to your staff.

❑ Explain how you will establish clear lines of communication up and down your chain of command.

❑ If your current position requires travel, state whether or not you are willing to continue to travel.

❑ Provide suggestions for handling overtime.

❑ If possible, outline methods for measuring your productivity under the new arrangement.

❑ Suggest a six-month review at which time both sides can submit an evaluation.

Step Four. Logistics: Include a logistical plan.

❑ Explain where you will do your work or how your office or computer could be utilized when you are out.

❑ Provide a detailed list of any additional equipment or materials you will need if you will be working at home or sharing a job.

Step Five. Salary and benefits: Make specific but reasonable requests for compensation.

❑ If your current position has full benefits, suggest a prorated version of the same.

❑ Negotiate a prorated salary, based on a full work week, commonly thirty-five or forty hours. (Some professional firms, however, calculate based on a fifty-hour week.)

❑ Hourly pay more often ensures you will be compensated for hours exceeding your formal arrangement. Be thorough.

Step Six. Summary: Be prepared to demonstrate in *business terms,* why this arrangement makes sense for your employer. Define how it serves your mutual interests.

❑ If possible, outline the costs and benefits to your employer and define any savings in terms of time, resources, or overhead costs.

In short, with this six-step approach you will want to think of every possible objection your supervisor might have and counter it with a solution. For example, if you think he or she will ask, "How do you expect to get the Friday summary report out if you plan to leave by noon?" be prepared with a well-thought-out and specific response. Say this: "I will reset the deadline for input from the field staff to Thursday at four and reserve Friday morning to complete the report by eleven."

It will be difficult to invalidate your position if you have well-thought-out answers to the most likely opposition.

FUEL FOR YOUR ARGUMENTS

If you think you will need extra ammunition, include facts like these that will solidify your case:

❏ *Demographics:* The shrinking labor force will cause smart companies to look for creative ways to keep good employees. Providing opportunities for flexible employment is one way to beat the shortage.

❏ *Replacement costs:* As the labor pool diminishes, the cost of replacing experienced and skilled employees will rise. Some analysts place the cost as high as one and a half times an employee's annual salary, in addition to whatever investments the company made in that person during their employment.

❏ *Productivity:* Most people in less-than-full-time jobs—particularly professionals—report that they are working smarter rather than longer. With fewer hours to get the job done, there is less time spent on casual conversation and nonessential activities. Further, these employees report to work fresh and relieved of their previous conflicts over balancing home and work.

❏ *Loyalty:* Many parents we interviewed reported a renewed sense of loyalty to the employer who provided a flexible work option for them.

❏ *Absenteeism:* Doctor visits, school conferences, and other personal appointments can be handled during time off rather than squeezed in during work hours.

❏ *Reduced turnover:* Many job-sharers and part-timers plan to return to work full-time when the demands of managing work and family lessen. Mothers facing the end of a maternity leave said they would not have returned to work had they not had a reduced schedule.

❏ *Recruiting power:* Companies like IBM, Proctor & Gamble, and Steelcase report that their commitment to work/family issues is a strong bargaining chip in their recruitment efforts.

❏ *Improved morale:* Although it's difficult to quantify, many of the holders of flexible jobs whom we interviewed reported an increased sense of well-being on the job and at home. Approximately 70 percent of the companies interviewed for the Catalyst study reported better morale among those who had switched to more flexible arrangements.

❏ *Turning innovation into income:* In 1983, university professor Rosabeth Moss Kantor and Goodmeasure, Inc., reported the findings of a study that compared the financial results over a twenty-year period of firms with and without innovative human resource practices. The innovators consistently came out ahead on more traditional measures of success, including sales, assets, and return on equity.

TIMING IS EVERYTHING

Choosing the right time, place, and method to make your proposal could make the difference between winning and losing your opportunity for flexibility.

Too Late. Don't choose the morning your baby-sitter arrived thirty minutes late and you are in a state of panic as the time to discuss this subject with your supervisor. "I waited until my back was up against the wall and I was totally desperate. My child-care situation was crumbling before I went in to talk to my boss about more flexibility," says Celia Farrell, an urban housing specialist with three children. "I walked into his office, sat down on the couch, and within thirty seconds started to cry.

"He was a very traditional man—the father of five, with a wife who had never worked. He took one look at me and said it was clear to him I belonged at home with my children."

Admitting his "old-fashioned attitudes," Farrell's boss refused her request for flexibility. In a paternalistic way, he suggested she find a way to stay home full-time.

Perhaps if Farrell had prepared herself better and approached her superior before she felt so desperate, she would have been able to lay out her plan more professionally and have received a different response.

Too Soon. Allison Young works four days a week as advertising manager for a western utility company. Her case illustrates how she avoided the disastrous results of making a request before being in a position to make a commitment.

"Before I proposed the part-time advertising job," explains Allison, "I was putting together a complete proposal to share a job with someone I knew very well. We had worked together for years. We were ready to go to management with the plan before she left on maternity leave. My gut told me we should wait, even though my co-worker was convinced she would be returning to work. Having just had a child myself, I knew that she didn't know what she was in for!

"I was glad we had not prematurely presented our concept, because Linda took one look at her daughter and decided not to return to work. I might have jeopardized my current flexible arrangement if I'd had to regroup and offer an alternative proposal."

Allison adds, "Your ninth month of pregnancy is not the ideal time to make another life-changing decision."

Not the Best Time. If your boss is under deadline pressure to submit budgets or to complete a major project, don't choose that time to come forward. If your company is the subject of a takeover, is pursuing an acquisition, or is in the process of downsizing, management's attention may be drawn elsewhere, and it may not be the best day to reorganize the department. In some circumstances, if you proceed with the appropriate knowledge and caution, the situation can work in your favor. For Jane Baker, the fact that her Phoenix company was cutting back was a benefit for her. When she approached her employer about turning a full-time position into part-time they viewed the situation as a problem solved. In their eyes they cut their costs in half and retained a highly prized employee.

Perfect Timing. Choose a time when you have reached a clear decision about your career. Know the amount of time you are willing to commit to the job you think will work for you and your company. If the organizational waters are relatively calm, use your best judgment to choose an occasion that will cast your proposal in the best possible light.

KNOWING WHAT TO SAY AND HOW TO SAY IT

This may be the first time your supervisor has dealt with the prospect of managing anything but a traditional work force. Be strategic in your approach, recognizing that you may be bringing a new concept to the table.

❑ *Be consistent.* If you regularly deliver formal proposals to the table, use all the structure we've provided. On the other hand, if you and your supervisor usually make decisions over lunch or even in the elevator, don't change your tactics now. Run through the exercise; have your backup in your back pocket. But, use the negotiating method that is tried and true for you.

❑ *Be professional.* It may be tempting to tell horror stories about the *worst* experiences you've had managing your work and a family. Avoid the temptation. Your employer may empathize with you. In fact, his or her lifestyle may be similar to yours, but there is a business to run. Make your pitch in terms he or she will appreciate. Business terms.

❑ *Avoid confrontation.* Some bosses may be inflexible and un-willing to consider alternative work options. Most will at least be willing to hear you out if you propose your idea in a positive way. A case presented without unreasonable demands or ulti-matums will most likely get a fair hearing.

❑ *Show your own flexibility.* Your boss may have a division to run or a tough quota to meet. Demonstrate that you are understand-ing of his goals and explain how your plan can assist, not assail, his efforts to reach them. If you think it will be necessary, explain your willingness to go beyond the boundaries of the job you've designed. For example, as part of our job-sharing agreement, Susan and I both agreed to attend important meetings on our days off. At the company's request, we both attended the annual convention.

The majority of parents we interviewed said that they occasionally worked beyond their designated hours and made a point of being available by phone at home.

❏ *Listen carefully.* Your supervisor may be unfamiliar with these new ways to work. Listen closely to his or her response to your proposal. If there are objections, perhaps they are merely a first response from someone steeped in traditionalism. Let him or her know that you will give some thought to the objections and will return with proposed solutions.

WHAT ABOUT BENEFITS?

Washingtonian Mary Sullivan retained full benefits when she scaled her association management job back from five days to four. Her employers considered it a perk provided to a valued employee.

Molly Madden received the value of her part-time benefits in cash from her Colorado Springs accounting firm. She then applied the funds to her husband's preexisting plan for better coverage.

In Pittsburgh, Cherie Kyl happily accepted her three-day-a-week public relations assignment without benefits. She felt the newfound job flexibility was worth the trade-off.

Just as the majority of flexible jobs we uncovered were negotiated between supervisor and employee, so it was with benefits. Meanwhile, the rising cost of providing benefits to employees has caused many companies to tighten the purse strings and request that even full-time employees make a greater contribution to the total cost of their plan. Others are offering "cafeteria style" programs, allowing staff to choose the benefits that best suit their needs.

Where flexible jobs are concerned, the most equitable approach for both employer and employee seems to be prorated benefits. For example, if you work half-time and receive half your original salary, then you would be eligible for half of all other benefits that apply to the full-time position, including vacation time and holidays. You may be able to negotiate the option to contribute the remainder of the full cost for health and life insurance and be fully covered.

Before you begin your negotiations, know what benefits

you can access through your spouse or other family members' policies or plans. Then, gather all the information available about your organization's policies. Compare your options. A human resources professional should be able to offer guidance.

Assess your own situation. Then make a pitch for what you need.

CLOSING THE DEAL

It may be tempting to take your flexibility and run. Don't be too eager. Your boss's negotiating strength lies in providing you with something he or she perceives you want badly. Flexibility shouldn't be considered a gift. Nor should it only be a reward for good performance. It should be provided on the basis that it makes sound business sense to do it. Throughout your negotiations, remember, *you* represent a valuable business asset.

With this in mind, keep the negotiating session open until the entire deal is done. Don't allow a sense of gratitude to sap your negotiating strength.

Make sure the following five points are resolved before you tie the bow around your new flexible package.

1. Have you discussed your current and future expectations for the job?
2. Have you discussed how special aspects of the job will be handled? For example, will you still be expected to travel? To attend planning meetings?
3. Have you clarified how overtime will be handled? Will you receive payment based on an hourly rate, or be provided compensatory time off? Will you be eligible for bonuses?
4. Discuss your promotability. Will you be eligible for promotions as a less-than-full-time employee? Some supervisors might assume you're content to sit tight unless you signal otherwise.
5. Do both you and your supervisor consider this flexible position permanent? Or is this a temporary experiment? Have you set a date for your next review?

Spending time on the details on the front end will save you headaches down the road. Lisa Jackson, a sales representative for an international service company, failed to negotiate overtime compensation when she crafted a three-day-a-week schedule. A few weeks into the new position, she was asked to travel to Europe for a ten-day sales blitz. Upon her return, she submitted a bill for the extra hours worked. It was rejected.

Her boss said she could take extra time off in the months ahead. The compensatory time, however, would not cover the extra child-care costs incurred as the result of her travel. "I was able to renegotiate payment for extra travel days in the future," says Jackson. "But I definitely had less negotiating power doing it after the fact."

Get your agreement in writing. If your supervisor doesn't take the initiative, you should. Then have your supervisor sign it. By having the details spelled out, you will be on solid footing should you have a change in management or any kind of misunderstanding.

By clarifying the issues *before* you accept the new position, you can avoid frustration and disappointment. A well-designed and workable flexible arrangement will bode well for your career and the future of flexibility within your organization.

8

TEN SUCCESSFUL
JOB STRATEGIES

There is no tried and true strategy for finding a flexible job. But there are lots of ways you can work it. In this chapter we look at the way ten individuals or pairs negotiated and then incorporated flexible work ways into their lives. They tell us why it worked, how it worked, and who helped them along the way.

KATE ROSE'S STORY

Growing up one of seven children in a middle-class New Jersey community, Rose and her siblings, full of the vigor that accompanied the 1960s, were determined to get ahead. "Everyone wanted to get off Lewis Street," she recalls.

They succeeded. Now when the family gathers for holidays they trade tales of professional challenge: two sisters are physicians, two are attorneys, one is in financial services. A brother is an engineer; the other, a New York investment banker. "When we looked to our future, we didn't think about working nine to five. We were going to change the world," remembers Rose. "We were shooting very high!"

But for Rose, her siblings, and friends who had children, reaching the heights with diaper bags on their shoulders has not been a joyride. That's why Rose left the partnership track at a high-powered, prestigious Washington, D.C., law firm to work instead for the government.

For the last nine years, this senior attorney and mother of three has moved in and out of the legal affairs division of the Federal Trade Commission, running investigations, doing trial work, and studying briefs—always less than full-time.

The FTC's liberal parental leave policy was a factor in pulling her in and keeping her there. Compared with what Rose might have encountered in private practice or on a corporate payroll, she had hit pay dirt. At the FTC employees with good work records can take up to a year, with supervisory approval, for parenting reasons—or, as some have, to do extended traveling, to go sailing, or to study paleontology.

After the birth of her first child, a daughter, Rose took six months off. "My supervisor thought that was adequate," she says. Later, when her son was born, with more seniority and savvy, she negotiated a seven-month leave; after her third child, she took ten months. In retrospect, she wishes she had taken the full year.

Rose believes that the FTC's flexible work policies have allowed the agency to attract a certain brand of individual who values personal freedom as much as work. Says Rose: "They know what we can make on the outside. So they've gotten creative with other kinds of compensation. They give us what they can to keep us: time."

To say that Rose's life is in perfect balance is not quite accurate. She and her husband, also an attorney, and their children teeter on a fine line between order and chaos. Add soccer games, baseball, and creative writing classes to the professional mix and things get wobbly. Her flexible job helps. His ability to be home each evening by six o'clock helps too.

Today, her schedule is this: Carpools fill the morning. After dropping off her youngest son, she parks the car, then reads aboard the Metro, barreling underground toward her downtown office. She's rarely in before ten. She's missed the morning warm-up; the office is in full swing. Her desk is piled with messages. The rest of her day is a blur. The return trip puts her at her front door about eight. She's missed the evening wind-down. Homework is under way. Tomorrow is Thursday, her day off.

How Rose logs the hours is up to her, as long as the total is thirty-two by week's end. "The general counsel's office doesn't care when I get there or when I leave, as long as the work gets done," says Rose. "Whether the hours are ten then six, twelve then eight; what matters is where you end up."

Sometimes the choices are hard. "I'd much rather get there at nine, so I wouldn't feel behind before I get started. But I really like taking Thomas to school," says Rose. "Sometimes he wants to show me around the room or we do a puzzle together. It's important time for both of us."

Going in late means trading off other things at day's end. "When we're running late and I walk in the door at nine P.M., that's hard. My children have things to talk about that shouldn't have had to wait that long."

When it gets too hard she takes off. Last summer she took a three-month leave. "I just started talking about it early. I had been working hard, long hours. I really needed a block of time to recover," recalls Rose. "We were losing one general counsel. Before he left I made the proposal. I got the approval and locked it in."

Hard-driving and professional, Rose savors the cooperative environment of her office. "In private firms, you can really shine at the expense of a colleague," she says. "Part of getting ahead is showing you are better than someone the firm thinks highly of. In government, you stand to gain more by working coop-eratively. You will help the person who is not there because you may need the same flexibility in your own career. You can work on a project and all get promoted together."

Still, she has mixed feelings about combining work and family. "It splits your personality," she says. "Everything's a compromise all the time. I enjoy my time at home. But I also get a lot of satisfaction from being in the middle of a big mess at work and solving it."

She doesn't like problem-solving enough to trade the financial rewards of private practice for the flexibility her current position allows. "I wouldn't work that way now, because I couldn't mother the way I want to mother. Even doing it this way is hard."

Most of the time her schedule—her life—works. She never really considers giving it up. The reason lies somewhere back on Lewis Street.

Why it works: Rose has been able to negotiate shortened hours as well as parental leaves during her tenure at the Federal Trade Commission. She has effectively studied her supervisors and has a clear understanding of their expectations. Consequently, she's entered negotiations confident that her proposals would meet with their approval. It is her firm belief that the quality of her work is highly valued by the agency. Day to day she has the full support of her colleagues. She has the added benefit of working in an environment with liberal policies about leave and shortened hours.

EILEEN MALLOY'S STORY

For Eileen Malloy, a Denver working mother, getting her daughter to preschool was a major stress inducer. Her employer expected her in the office from 8:30 until 5:00, but Megan's preschool didn't begin until 9:00. The baby-sitter was trustworthy, but Malloy didn't feel comfortable sending her daughter in the sitter's less-than-reliable car. A single mother, Malloy couldn't look to her husband to help resolve the problem. Nor could she afford to risk losing her job as media relations manager for a consumer products company.

As winter approached, the prospect of icy roads loomed. Her uneasiness about the transportation situation nagged at her each morning; Megan could sense it.

"It just didn't seem right," remembers Malloy. "I knew there had to be a way I could fulfill both responsibilities without sacrificing in either case." She analyzed her work situation and realized that if she took Megan to school herself, not only would she eliminate the daily worry (another mom agreed to bring her daughter home), but she would have the chance to get to know the teacher and some of Megan's friends. That was important too. Things were normally pretty slow in the office before ten. The crunch always seemed to come at the end of the day.

She drafted a plan and presented it to her supervisor. It included these suggestions: Eileen would call into the office at 8:30, provide her assistant with morning assignments (that would get the ball rolling), and check the updated schedule for the day. She agreed to handle important media calls or any crisis before departing for Megan's classroom at 8:50. Driving to school, dropping off her daughter, and returning to the office would take less than forty-five minutes. Malloy would be at her desk no later than 9:45.

In exchange for this early-morning flexibility, Malloy would work until six each evening and cut fifteen minutes from her lunch hour. Her salary and benefits package would not change because the number of hours she worked would stay the same.

Her boss approved the plan, recognizing that, in fact, more of their crisis work took place in the evening. It would be nice, he admitted, to have an extra hand at the end of the day.

Now that the new schedule is under way, mornings in the Malloy household are considerably more pleasant. Megan is less anxious about going to school, picking up on her mother's newfound enthusiasm for their morning ritual. While phone calls from the office sometimes pierce the mood, Malloy considers it a welcome trade-off.

Later, at the office, Malloy can dive right into work knowing that her daughter has arrived safely at school. "I don't have any objective way to measure it, but I think my productivity is way up," says Malloy. "Now I can focus on my work straightaway. I don't have to wonder. I have peace of mind."

Why it works: Malloy found that by shifting her hours in a way that actually proved beneficial to her department, she was able to solve a problem that had seemed insurmountable. She analyzed her situation and then presented a well-thought-out plan that allowed her to keep her full salary and benefits.

SEAN AND BECKY GRIFFIN'S STORY

Sean and Becky Griffin made a very important decision, based on casual observation. "Before we had children we were both working hard and it seemed like over our shoulders someone was always telling a disastrous child-care story," remembers Sean. "At first, I didn't pay much attention. It was someone else's problem. But the closer we got to having children, the louder the voices became."

By the time their first daughter was born, both parents had decided they would leave the business of child care to no one else. "We weren't sure how it would work out," says Sean. "But somehow we intended to be primary caregivers to our children."

Sean covers Washington for the *Phoenix Gazette*—a one-man bureau. Becky is a copy editor for the *Washington Post*, working from 4:30 until midnight an average of three nights a week.

With Sean working days and Becky on nights they were on the right track for their unorthodox approach to child care. There was one problem. The schedules left two hours—4:30 until 6:30 P.M.—when neither parent was available.

Here's how they closed the gap: Sean called his editor in Phoenix and candidly explained his situation—the couple wanted to avoid a dependence on child care and he needed some help. Could he cut his nine-to-five day in the office short and then file his story by modem from home each evening? "That way Becky could drop the baby off at the office on her way to the *Post*. I could take her home and put her to bed. Then I'd work till midnight," says Sean.

"At first there was a little hesitation on the other end of the phone line," recalls Sean. "It was difficult for them to swallow. She said things like 'We haven't done this kind of thing before.' But within a few days I had the green light."

Sean found late-night duty had its rewards. "It is easier to reach people at home at night. I'm not just another pink slip stacking up during the day, a person among twenty waiting for a few words of wisdom from a source." Consequently, he comments, "people are more relaxed; they have time to think and are more willing to talk."

There are other times, Sean notes, when he has had to interview a member of Congress with "the sound of a baby in the background as well as a keyboard."

Still, three months after the new schedule was under way, his city editor called to say, "Things are going fine. You're still churning out the copy."

For Becky's part, she's tired a lot. But, she says, the fatigue that comes with going to bed at 2:00 A.M. and getting up again with small children at 7:00 is part of their program. Unquestionably it's worth the sleep they sacrifice. Adds Becky: "There's this certain feeling between us that the quality of what we're doing is very, very good."

The Griffins began working this way in 1986. When their son was born two years later the "hand-off" became a little trickier, but still possible. The "adventure" of getting home involves meeting Becky under the awning of the National Press Building, where she passes along instructions as well as children. Sean puts Benjamin in the backpack, takes Halle by the hand, and heads for the Metro. Then comes the shuffle for fare cards and finding a place for "two and a half people to sit." They transfer to a bus at National Airport; in total, an hour passes before they reach their front door.

"It is cumbersome; the parka, the umbrellas, the occasional tug of war," says Sean. "But I think the kids actually enjoy passing the window displays with flashing lights, magazine stands with candy and toys, funny-looking people—the street theater that adults take for granted.

"We both look at it as though we have one-and-a-half full-time jobs—parent and primary caregiver—in addition to the jobs that pay our salaries," Sean says. "I can't think of a single thing that has been better for my self-esteem than being a dad my children can depend on. There are so many rewards and opportunities involved with relying on your hunches and instincts, solving your children's problems and doing it right."

Washington, D.C., ranks among the top ten of the most expensive places in the United States to live—one reason more two-career couples live there than anywhere else in the U.S. Consequently, Sean and Becky have considered a move to a city where they can live more comfortably on one salary. Ideally, they would like to share a job.

"For now," says Sean, "our arrangement is not perfect, but it's workable. And I think when you mix work with family, flexibility is the best you can hope for."

Why it works: This couple was able to combine his telecommuting, or work at home, with her part-time position to effectively eliminate any child-care concerns. Sean was able to gain the long-term support of his editor by actually improving the quality of his work. Both he and Becky have always been conscientious workers, instilling confidence in their employers. The work load provided by both employers can be handled adequately within the time frames set.

CAROLYN BOWMAN'S AND MARGO EWING'S STORY

It is not surprising that some teachers suffer from burnout. Whining. Runny noses. Excuses. Pushy parents. But for Carolyn Bowman, teaching in Southern California was a way of life and she loved it—until she had kids of her own.

"It just didn't work out the way I had planned it," says Bowman, who waited until age thirty-eight to have her first child. "I would pick up my children at the sitter's after a day in the classroom and I was pooped! I had used up all my energy. My own children were numbers thirty-two and thirty-three on the priority list. And my husband? He got what few crumbs were left over."

One evening over dinner Bowman's husband, also an educator, told her about their district's new superintendent. With Dr. Sanchez came an innovative way to keep teachers from leaving. He called it partnering. We know it as job-sharing. "That news made it possible for me to survive the year," says Bowman.

She immediately began the search for the right teaching partner. Through mutual friends she hooked up with a woman whose teaching philosophy she shared. They made a proposal to the school district and it was accepted. Bowman was elated. Then she got the phone call. Her partner was pregnant; no pregnant partners were allowed. Hugely disappointed, she was back at square one.

Through the school system, Bowman tracked down three women who were returning from maternity leave. She called Margo Ewing. "We hit it off immediately," says Bowman.

They developed a plan molded around the few guidelines set by the district. For example, they couldn't just split the year in half and each teach a semester. They decided to alternate weeks, beginning on each Thursday. Both would teach everything with these exceptions: Ewing had the musical talent; Bowman knew language arts. Ewing would teach social science; Bowman would take on science. Shortly after applying, they received their fourth-grade teaching assignment. That was seven years ago.

They complement each other. If one is stumped on what to do with the bulletin boards, the other insists on "primary colors." An early morning phone call might mean one partner is sick. If possible, the healthy one will substitute. They leave notes and keep each other informed. They both show up for meetings, holiday parties, and the school play.

What do the students say about job sharing? "They think Mrs. Bowman is funny and Mrs. Ewing is nice," says Bowman (who *is* funny). "They tell us they never get bored, because they have *two teachers*." Bowman adds: "On Thursday, I might hear 'Mrs. Ewing, Mrs. Ewing!' I call them Herman until they get the idea and laugh."

And the parents' reactions? One moved his child for "continuity" reasons. Another transferred a son because of a basic personality conflict. "Oh, we've had them say things like 'Janey is scared of you but not Mrs. Ewing,' or vice versa. But generally I think they recognize they are getting good energy from both of us. We get requests for our classroom," Bowman says.

Educators aren't known for their prosperity, and sometimes getting just half of a teacher's salary can be tough. Says Bowman: "We pay to have the house cleaned only during the weeks I teach." Their paychecks reflect their seniority. Each gets half of what their full-time salary would be. They both receive prorated benefits.

Why it works: Bowman and Ewing job-share a position that has been split to capitalize on their individual strengths and interests. They have developed a longstanding professional and supportive relationship with one another, the fruits of which are a gift to their students. They communicate well. Their negotiations were simplified by the support of the district superintendent. The current support of their principal provides continued security to the arrangement.

SHARON WOODSIDE'S STORY

For a good part of the year, accounting employees wear dark circles under their eyes. Deadlines are constant; late nights, routine. If you like the work, life inside a national public accounting firm is good. But it doesn't leave much energy for life on the outside. At least that's what Sharon Woodside found.

As her second year with the Kansas City firm came to a close, she was expecting her first child. Another woman accountant had resigned; for her, the pressure and long hours didn't mix with motherhood. Woodside shared those concerns. The partners called her colleague at home and offered reduced hours if she would return. That gave Woodside hope.

"She really paved the way for me," recalls Woodside. While on maternity leave, she telephoned the partner in charge of the tax department and negotiated her own flexible job. Eight hours a day, three days a week.

But even though her hours had changed, the culture of the firm had not. "They still expected me to stay as long as it took to get the work done the days I was in the office," remembers Woodside. "There were some people who understood my situation; others did not. They said family was important, but they really didn't mean it."

So why stay? thought Woodside. Family *was* important to her. With the ink barely dry on her master's degree in accounting, she knew she had enough experience and education to go out and get an equivalent job—or better. So she did.

What was she looking for? No weekends. No late nights. Not more than twenty hours a week outside of tax season. Without giving up the security of her current job, she began the search. She talked to her professors, friends, and professional acquaintances. Surprisingly, she found many women who had been in her shoes. They offered guidance. She examined their choices. "I thought about starting my own firm, but I didn't think I had enough experience. I thought about teaching, but the pay isn't too good," says Woodside. "I talked with parents who were doing both." The most encouraging reports came from women who worked for small accounting firms with the "right management."

Woodside believed this to be an important *career* decision. She would take her time. "I talked with one woman who worked from her home. She was retiring and was willing to give me her client list. It was tempting. But I wanted to get stronger in the tax area, to specialize. I made the decision to stick with my search."

She interviewed for several full-time positions, explaining her terms to management. She got close, but there was never the right fit. "I had decided what I wanted and I would keep looking until I found it," recalls Woodside. "I was always very up-front."

The newspaper offered her next lead: *Wanted: full-time tax accountant. Small firm.* That same day the phone rang; it was a headhunter. He was charged with filling a job—the same one she had circled in the paper. A few hours later, her professor called. "Just heard about a position that sounds right for you," he said. It was the same job. It must have had her name on it.

She interviewed with the firm's partners, explaining that her goal was to work about 50 percent of the year. She recognized there would be a higher concentration of hours during tax season. "I would be flexible too," she told them. It was an idea they had never considered.

Woodside sold them on the bottom line, an appropriate strategy for one accountant to use with another. "I have experience. I'll be there when you need me," Woodside explained. "When you don't need me, you won't be paying expensive talent to sit in the office." They hired her over others who had applied for the full-time position.

An employment agreement was signed that included the following: The parties decided on a twenty-hour work week, although both agreed to be flexible. Woodside's hours would be Monday through Thursday, 9:00 A.M. until 2:00 P.M. During tax season—the three months prior to April 15—she would work forty hours a week if necessary, but no more. She would be compensated at an hourly rate for any hours worked beyond the agreement. Other accountants would be hired to fill in the gaps. During the slow season she could take additional time off without pay. The firm could not offer her benefits at twenty hours; instead, they gave her the prorated value of the benefits—about $500—in cash each month.

The arrangement works well. Most projects have a two-week turnaround. There is challenge, but seldom crisis. "I much prefer this situation to the pressure cooker I left," says Woodside. "I am much more relaxed. There is more energy for my family and for work."

Why it works: In her first flexible position, Woodside found that, despite lip service to a policy, the culture of the firm was not supportive. Now she enjoys the full support of a management group that understands the business benefit to their firm. An employment agreement provides clarity. She was able to create her own opportunity by carefully defining what she wanted and setting her own goals. Through effective use of her professional contacts she was able to research the available options and make an informed choice.

COLLEEN CLARK'S STORY

After a day in the Denver office, Colleen Clark heads south, away from the city. This stretch of highway is nearly hers alone; she commutes at off hours to avoid the rush. As the odometer tracks the miles toward home, Pikes Peak comes into view. A rock, a large rock, twisted like a castle, guards the town where she lives. It is rightfully called Castle Rock. The closer she gets, the more relaxed she becomes. She won't be going to the office again for a few days. But she'll be working. At home. She's a telecommuter.

Almost six years ago, Clark had the first of her three children. As her maternity leave neared its end, the thought of returning to her engineering job caused genuine panic. "I never thought it would be so hard," remembers Clark. "Every time I thought about leaving the baby I started to cry." She started back on a part-time basis, but before long US West needed her full-time input.

"At that point, I seriously thought about resigning," says Clark, now thirty. "I really hesitated to do it because engineering changes constantly. It would be very difficult to play catch-up later. But before I got very far my supervisor said, 'If you're thinking about quitting, hold on. Maybe we can transfer you into a different job, use your training, and have you at home.' "

Not wanting to lose Clark, her managers swiftly switched her responsibilities with another engineer's; within two weeks she was communicating by computer from Castle Rock. The first month she received a raise and a bonus.

Now she works forty hours a week, mostly from her basement office. She goes to the company's Denver office for special meetings. But often she runs through a meeting agenda at home, using a speaker phone to do conference calls. Or she works on her computer, studying data sheets and interference studies. While the company prefers that telecommuters work two or three days in the office ("We want our employees connected to the business," says Mike Dillon, US West's personnel manager), they have left scheduling to Clark's discretion. She makes the trip to Denver once a week.

The company offers a training course to help telecommuters and their supervisors foresee problems and adjust easily to the new workstyle. One recommendation is that employees not try to do two jobs at once: in this case, engineering and child care. Clark has a full-time baby-sitter in her home, but she breaks for lunch and snacks with the children.

"There are times when they play outside my office," says Clark. "But when the door is closed they know I'm working. The important thing is they know I am home." Some days she begins her work before dawn so they can all spend late afternoons together.

Virtually every study of telecommuting reports isolation as a potential down side to this work option. But Clark, bolstered by the opportunity to spend more time with her children, says that for her it's not a problem. She talks several times a week with other telecommuters and communicates with friends and co-workers via her computer-based fax.

In some companies, out of sight could mean out of mind when promotions are passed out. But at U S West, the program has strong management support. "I don't think I would be passed over," says Clark. "I have a very good rapport with my boss and his boss."

Performance reviews aren't a problem, in part because Clark's productivity is easily measured. She has her own territory and must meet a quota of sorts as well as constant FCC deadlines. "There is no room to slip up," she says. In fact, during the first year she worked at home, her output increased 33 percent. "At home, I'm more relaxed. There are so few interruptions. No idle conversation. No one coming in to ask questions. I just get a lot more done," reports Clark.

Clark's friends and neighbors think her work situation is so ideal she must have taken a pay cut. But, of course, because she is a full-time employee, her salary and benefits stay the same. For Clark, the work situation is ideal. "I count my blessings," she says.

Why it works: Clark's telecommuting position fits handily within the guidelines U S West has developed for its program. The arrangement allows her to keep pace in a fast-changing profession. Clark has a well-defined task, the results of which are measurable. Her productivity, therefore, is easily monitored. She enjoys a good working relationship with her supervisor and co-workers and receives their full cooperation. While isolation can be a problem for other telecommuters, Clark sees her ability to remain at home with her children as a substantial asset. Her morale is high.

ANN SALIERS'S AND PEGGY HOOGERHYDE'S STORY

Saliers's and Hoogerhyde's job-sharing arrangement is representative of what is happening in the most progressive companies. The two women share a full-time job as consultants in corporate sales support for Steelcase, a midwestern manufacturing company. Their joint résumé made them stand out in the eyes of the supervisor who hired them.

Before their job-share they had known each other as friends and co-workers. In fact, their relationship developed through snatches of conversation exchanged in the home of the baby-sitter whose services they both used. One day, their conversation turned to job-sharing. Hoogerhyde, pregnant with her second child, wanted to spend less time on the job. Saliers, who shortened her hours after the birth of her first child, was willing to consider a change. The more they talked, the more it made sense. They began to strategize. Their skills, personalities, and experience were complementary. They hoped a company manager would agree.

Fortunately for the pair, job-sharing is an accepted practice at Steelcase. They didn't have to sell the concept, only themselves. How would they differentiate themselves from other single applicants? Could they position their partnership as an asset?

They decided to write a joint résumé, putting all their strengths onto one document. With both names at the top, they listed their experience and accomplishments in chronological order. Together, they had eighteen years of experience with the company, an MBA in marketing and human resources and undergraduate degrees in architecture and interior design. For a company that designs, manufactures, and markets office furniture, their completed résumé had genuine punch.

Next they met with the employee relations manager. The threesome reviewed the available positions. Saliers and Hoogerhyde chose four in which there was mutual interest.

The employee relations manager served as front man, meeting ahead of time with managers to determine their interest in talking with the team. Interviews were scheduled for three of the four targeted positions.

"We really believed we brought more to the job than any single person could," says Saliers. "It was like hiring a first and third baseman for the price of one other player."

They were offered, together, the position of senior consultant in corporate sales support. Here's their arrangement: They each work half-time; Saliers works Monday and Wednesday, Hoogerhyde on Tuesday and Thursday. They alternate Fridays. Each receives half the full-time salary and half the benefits, with the option of obtaining full-cost medical benefits for a small monthly fee. They are reviewed by their supervisor independently.

Two years into their job-share, both Hoogerhyde and Saliers are satisfied. They work hard at communicating with each other and with co-workers. "The burden is on us to make sure communication happens with co-workers and clients," says Saliers. "We don't want to make it more difficult for those we work with; we never say, 'Call back when she's here.' We pass the message on."

"At times we suffer from information overload," says Saliers. "To be good at what we do, we have to keep up with full-time information in half as many hours. It can make the time in the office very intense."

Both women are interested in training and see it as important to assuring promotion. That is, according to Saliers, one of the challenges of sharing a job: "It's very difficult to convey to another person what you learned in a seminar. But in our situation, it is hard to justify both attending."

Both women believe they *should* be eligible for a promotion as a team. It has happened before at Steelcase. "If a position opened up, I would hope we would be just as much a candidate as any other individual," says Saliers.

Why it works: These two women have been able to stay on track, a priority for both, in a professional position because of their job-sharing arrangement. They used creativity and initiative in their application process by developing a joint résumé; the strategy immediately proved their ability to innovate and work together. Their partnership works well. They communicate regularly and provide constant professional support to one another. Further, they have the strong support of their company at all levels.

ELEANOR FRIEDMAN'S STORY

You've seen it on prime-time television: serious-looking people, in serious clothes; clearly, they are doing serious work and making serious money. It is *LA Law*.

So what happens in real life when a major player decides that just maybe her children, her family, are more important than the client, any client?

This is the story of a woman who made it through an Ivy League law school and into one of the nation's most prestigious law firms, only to discover that parenting paid bigger rewards than partnership.

She was in; now, with a few years of hard work, she would be made partner. She was sure of it—until she got pregnant. "As each month of the pregnancy passed the decision became increasingly more difficult," remembers Eleanor Friedman. "I just couldn't see myself having a young baby and working that many hours."

Fortunately for Friedman, her Los Angeles firm had a policy that enabled lawyers to reduce their hours if desired. But for a woman as intense as Friedman, the decision was excruciating. "I agonized over it," she recalls. "But I decided that I would ask them for a part-time position. At the same time I prepared myself to quit if they said no; I would just go do something else with my life."

They said yes. And much to Friedman's surprise, what she thought would be a formal negotiating session was casual conversation in the hallway. "The firm's senior partner asked me what I thought I would do," says Friedman, who was seven months pregnant at the time. " 'I am really not sure,' I told him. 'I think I'd like to work part-time.' His response was: 'You just tell me what you want and we'll work it out.' The question came in such an off-hand way," continued Friedman. "But I had given it so much thought, I just took the opportunity to say it."

After the birth of her child she began working 60 percent of full-time, or three days a week. Soon she had inched her way up to 70 and then 80 percent. She was billing so many hours her reviewing partner "became somewhat embarrassed at what I was being paid compared to what I was billing." Two years later, after the birth of her second child, she dropped back to 70 percent.

In this firm, like most others, working shortened hours means stepping off the partnership track. To once again be considered for partner, a lawyer must work full-time for two years. "They kept telling me if I went back on track I could still be flexible. I wouldn't have to bill any more hours than I was in the part-time arrangement," remembers Friedman. "I decided to see if that was true."

She was approaching the magic date—the beginning of the twelve-month review period after which new partners are tapped. "I looked ahead at what the next year would be like and asked myself, What is important?" remembers Friedman. "I had all the support at work; they kept telling me I was wonderful, that I deserved to make partner. But on the other hand, I knew I would be trading off my family if I chose to really go for it."

Part of Friedman's dilemma was looking down the road at life in the partner's overstuffed chair. Realistically, that meant long hours and weekends. And lots of money. "They said, 'We are flexible; we know you have kids. No one will say anything if you're not around as much,'" says Friedman. "I had two problems with that: I'd heard that story before and I'm not sure it is realistic; and, second, it doesn't fit with the kind of person I am. I knew I would think, If this is my business I must put in as much work as my colleagues."

She went to management and took herself off the partnership track—again. But this time she proposed a new idea: Would they consider the concept of a part-time partner? "That blew everybody's mind; they weren't ready for it," says Friedman. "I thought if any firm would go for it, this one would. But it was too soon."

Instead, they offered her the position of attorney, of

counsel to the firm, a position that carries a title and ranks above the associate level. Friedman accepted.

No doubt her arrangement is the envy of other lawyers. She works 70 percent of a full-time schedule, logging the hours any way she chooses. Most days, work begins at 9:45 and ends at 5:30; often she leaves at 2:00 and takes the kids to a museum or to the park. (There are four: two of her own and two stepchildren.) She works an occasional weekend. She participates in management groups. For her efforts, Friedman receives full benefits and takes home a salary she says is "more than that of many partners in other law firms" in the same city.

Passing up partnership has meant occasional awkward moments at negotiating tables and not "running deals." She could make more money. But she and her family do well by almost any standard on her current salary plus what her husband, also a lawyer, brings home.

Her professional voice softens when she talks about what the changes in her schedule have meant to her children. "They get more love and attention from Mom now," she says. "I see the look on their faces when I come home early. They are pretty happy kids."

Why it works: Friedman is comfortable with her decision to work shortened hours and to forgo partnership for the near future. The work is interesting and challenging and she has the full support of the partners. Through their flexibility, they were able to retain her valuable services. She believes she is well compensated and has retained full benefits.

PAT QUINN CASPER'S AND HANNEKE DEEKEN'S STORY

It is not surprising that the position was tough to fill. As Pat Quinn Casper puts it: "Pediatric hospice is not a big draw." The question before Casper and colleague Hanneke Deeken was this: Did the Milwaukee Children's Hospital want to fill it badly enough to experiment? Would they hire a job-sharing team?

Casper had seen the job posted in the hospital where she was already employed. She knew a little about hospice work, enough to know it was a job she didn't want to handle on her own. Word was that this particular position would be more challenging than usual; it needed a facelift, fresh insight.

Perhaps her old workmate Deeken was ready to return to the hospital. It had been twelve years since they had worked together as neophyte floor nurses in a chemotherapy unit. Since then, both had moved from Milwaukee, married, and had children. Now they were both back on Lake Michigan's shores. She called to find out.

"I was feeding my newborn baby," remembers Deeken. "The whole time she was talking, I half listened and thought to myself, It's too soon to go back—I won't work till this child is in school. Then something she said broke through. Job-sharing."

Deeken automatically assumed job-sharing meant a fifty-fifty split. It wasn't until Casper suggested an eighty-twenty split that Deeken's interest was piqued. "That was manageable," she said.

This was their opportunity. The pediatric hospice program was badly in need of repair; every aspect needed a redesign. Add the emotional and physical strain and long hours imposed by hospice work and you had a white elephant of a job. Still, it was a position the hospital wanted to fill with the right person, one who could turn the program around.

As two master's-prepared clinical nurses with complementary interests and experience, they had the right credentials. They also had the physical and mental stamina between them to take on such a trying task.

"We asked ourselves how many times would we get the chance to develop a program, do research at a professional level, and still be home for the school bus," said Casper.

They decided to apply for the position together. First they agreed they would shape the job around their personal lives. For now, while Deeken's children were small, she would work 20 percent of the hours; Casper would work 80 percent. As their family situations changed (Casper planned to have another child), things would even out.

They submitted an application along with their résumés; then they spent a month and a half on the legwork, researching the current hospice program as well as other job-sharing examples. "We went through the pros and cons. We talked about why job-sharing would be appropriate for us and the hospital," recalls Casper.

They decided to downplay the fact that they were both mothers who wanted to work shortened hours. Rather, they would focus on the benefits to the hospital and to nursing.

By the time of their first interview, they were well rehearsed. "We took turns answering questions. They needed to know we had talked through every aspect of the job," says Casper. "If one of us glared at the other, that meant 'I'm stuck. Please say something.' We wanted to show we could operate as a team." It took twelve interviews, but they got the job.

Together they share the responsibility of caring for dying children and their grieving families. Because of the emotional stress, it is a job better shared than held by one. They make visits at all hours of the day and night to their patients' homes; 90 percent of their patients end their young lives there.

As their own lives changed (Casper has had another child), their hours have evened out. It works better that way. There was a time when Casper's high profile, by virtue of her additional hours, made for uncomfortable moments. "It hit me on two levels," recalls Deeken. "She was the identifiable person. They all sort of adopted Pat as the head of the program. By default I became the 'assistant head.' Sometimes I felt bad about it. But I always held on to the fact that my time would come. As my hours have increased the problem has diminished."

Today, they split the job along the lines of their strengths. Says Casper, "Hanneke is the thinker, I am the doer." They communicate by phone, through notes, and during their shared hours. They leave extensive messages, using the hospital's voice mail system. Rarely is a program decision made without input from both.

The hospital is pleased with their performance and the job-share is considered a success. Deeken and Casper are satisfied too; they have given new life to the children's hospice program.

Why it works: The two proved themselves to be capable and innovative during the negotiating process. Their thorough research and intense preparation won them the job. Currently, they are fastidious in their communication with each other, believing the effort keeps the partnership healthy. They are themselves flexible, always mindful of the other's personal and professional needs. They have been given both support and autonomy by the hospital, reflecting the institution's faith in their integrity and work.

NANCY MADISON'S STORY

Nancy Madison had good solid experience. She'd cracked the big egg right out of school, landing a job with a New York advertising agency. Sure, it was entry level, but it was an impressive launch for a young woman from a sleepy Georgia town. Now with ten years' experience, a move to Orlando, and award-winning work behind her, she was ready for a break-through of another kind—finding a position that would mesh with motherhood.

Much to her own surprise, Madison didn't want to give up her career. She enjoyed the ad business: the creative challenge, scurrying to meet deadlines, schmoozing with clients. Now that she had a daughter she wanted to find a way to enjoy both career and parenting.

Hoping to cash in on her six years of seniority, Madison had tried to work something out with her then employer. The first go-round produced results. They agreed to a twenty-hour-a-week schedule. But within a few months, a management shuffle left her with a full-time work load on a part-time salary.

"I was handling seven acounts," relates Madison. "There was no way anyone could accomplish the goals they set in under sixty hours a week. They were getting senior work for no money."

Madison tried to renegotiate a more equitable arrange-ment. "It was clear they weren't interested in flexibility," she recalls. "Finally, they said it was their way or no way. So, I quit."

Madison hadn't looked for a job since those early days in New York. Opportunity had always come to her. At least now she had a deep well of professional contacts on which to draw.

Recently, she had run into Elizabeth Randon, an alumna of her former agency. Randon had started her own firm. Madison gave her a call.

The timing was perfect. Randon's new agency was taking off. She had no problem obtaining a willing crew of inexperienced youth; it was senior talent Randon was scrambling to find. Her start-up company could not yet afford to pay top salaries. Hiring Nancy Madison was her answer.

They shaped this schedule: Madison works three days a week, managing accounts from 9:30 until 3:30. If the agency's work load increases, her hours can too. "If a client needs something extra I can work as much as is necessary," says Madison. "At the same time, if my child is sick, I take off and make it up another day. It's unbelievably flexible.

"Clients may have the perception that if we are not there all the time we don't care about them," says Madison. "So I go out of my way to be available and to get things done on time. I am a lot more conscientious about managing my time at work."

Madison gets tremendous support from others at the agency. "They are willing to tailor their needs to meet mine," she says. "It's an attitudinal difference. They say, 'You are here these hours and we will work to make things happen when you're around.'"

There are times she has to limit herself because of the reduced hours. "From a growth standpoint I can't always pursue things—new business for the agency or my own professional development," says Madison. "But that's my choice. I had to slow down on one track or the other; and my primary commitment is to my family."

Why it works: This is clearly a win/win situation. With shortened hours, Madison keeps her foot in the professional door and still has time for her family; Randon has access to high-level talent while her agency grows. There is an atmosphere of mutual respect.

9

ON THE JOB: MAKING FLEXIBILITY WORK

The parents we interviewed for this book are special. Enthusiastic self-starters, many seem to sense that being part of this first wave of workplace flexibility is somehow important. They take pride in going against the grain, for innovating in a conservative realm. And they believe in themselves.

The need for that somewhat courageous spirit goes beyond taking a gutsy approach to negotiating. Making your flexible job work will require special skills; after all, you are a pioneer. Here's how to get started.

FIRST STEPS

Securing Management Support. We found the most successful flexible arrangements inside companies with supportive policies or under a particularly supportive manager. Such arrangements are *openly* negotiated and kept in the open.

Flexibility that is shrouded in secrecy is doomed from the start. Often, a sympathetic supervisor quietly extends flexibility without the sanction of superiors. Employees in this awkward situation view their jobs as special favors or interim arrangements to be disposed of at the whim of a single supervisor.

Productivity is nearly impossible if you fear for the future of your job. To eliminate the stress of such uncertainty, solidify the support of the people who count. If you did not get your flexible arrangement in writing during the negotiating process, do it now. It doesn't have to be a long document; in most cases, it will fit on a single page. This piece of paper will give you peace of mind and perhaps protect your flexible job if management changes.

Let the human resources department know about your arrangement. If you encounter snags, their support may help you. They may ask you to document your experiences, or talk with others considering a similar workstyle. If you are among the first to try it, your success will strengthen their case for further flexibility.

Communicating with Your Supervisor. The negotiating process probably provided a good start toward defining your responsibilities. But once you're on the job, it is worthwhile to revisit the specifics. Talk with your supervisor about how you will handle work assignments, problem-solving, and progress reports. What will his or her expectations be for days when you are out of the office? Will you be expected to call in or be available by phone? If you are telecommuting, will you be expected to provide any written reports?

Confirm the time frame after which you will review the arrangement. In the interim don't hesitate to address any glitches directly.

Explain Your Arrangement to Co-workers. You'll get a lot more support from co-workers if they clearly understand the structure of your job. Ask your supervisor to put together a memo outlining your new hours and explaining your responsibilities. If you find resistance, write the memo yourself. Ask your supervisor to sign it and distribute it to the appropriate people. Include everyone you work with, no matter how infrequently. Make sure the memo includes the hours and/or days you will be working in the office. If you will be working and available at home, include that information too. This will put everyone at ease.

A message from your supervisor will also eliminate the possibility of someone misconstruing your change in schedule. "After I started working three days a week," recalls a thirty-two-year-old marketing director, "I thought it was odd that no one commented on my schedule. It wasn't until after a story about my new schedule ran in our employee paper that I discovered everyone thought I'd been demoted."

Consider asking the editor of your employee paper or newsletter to write a feature story about your flexible job. A positive article will clarify your arrangement and perhaps encourage some of your colleagues who might be considering a similar career move. But first make sure that management approves publicizing your arrangement.

Determine with whom you will be working closely. What information or feedback will they need from you? At what intervals? Will they need to reach you on your days off? Will you be able to communicate easily via home computer, courier, or fax?

In staff meetings, provide thorough updates of your work in progress. Put important project information on paper and distribute it as a resource for those times when you are not present.

Communicating with Clients and Associates. Be sure your work arrangement is communicated properly to people calling from outside your department or company. You don't want your business associates to get the impression you are hard to reach.

Take Advantage of Training. Companies like Aetna, Time Inc., Steelcase, and J. C. Penney provide training on the subject of managing alternative work arrangements. At U S West, where shortened hours and telecommuting are encouraged, both parties to a flexible arrangement are required to spend a full day learning how to make the arrangement successful. A training video tape was made for employees in remote locations who found it hard to get to a session. If your company makes the offer, take them up on it.

Scores of good books and articles have been written about virtually every aspect of flexible jobs. (Some are listed in the Bibliography of this book.) Share them with your supervisor.

NOW YOU'RE UP AND RUNNING

Square Peg, Round Hole? So much to do, so little time. If that's how you feel, look carefully at the assignment you've undertaken. Make sure you can do the job well in the time you've committed.

Carolyn Brodie, a thirty-three-year-old market researcher in Baltimore, was eager to spend more time at home; she convinced her boss she could accomplish five days' worth of work in four. Before long she found herself exhausted trying to fulfill her promise. "I was so frustrated," recalls Brodie. "I set myself up. Rather than get the break I was looking for, I ended up staying late and taking work home. My off day became a work day." After six months Brodie admitted to the flaw in her plan. She renegotiated with her employer to pass on one-fifth of her work to a colleague.

A few extra hours may come with the territory. But if you find you've committed to too much, the time to renegotiate is now. You and your supervisor should be sorting this new arrangement out together. Keep him or her informed of your ability to fulfill your commitment.

Learning to Say No. In the fall of 1988, I, Lynn, cut my schedule back to three days—I worked Monday, Wednesday, and Friday. On the evening before I was to take my first day off, I received a call from Bob Hazard, the president of my company. We talked about a project he wanted me to work on. The conversation ended with his suggestion that we meet the following morning to discuss the issue further. I cringed in my chair, said "Fine," and hung up. For a moment I was disappointed, thinking I was about to work through my first day off. I wasn't accustomed to saying no to this man. But I knew I had to learn.

Within minutes, I picked up the phone and called him back. I said, "I forgot for a moment that tomorrow my shortened schedule goes into effect. I won't be in the office. Would a Wednesday morning meeting work on your calendar?"

There was a slight pause at the other end of the line. "That would be fine," he said. "See you Wednesday." That was the first of many similar conversations. Each time it got easier. Eventually, people began asking me which days would be convenient for me to meet.

The difficult assignment of taking on less rather than more is yours alone. Stick to your schedule from the very beginning. Your colleagues will take their cue from you. But if they sense you are willing to work extra hours, or to leave your telecommuting site to attend regular meetings in the office, they will push.

More often, however, it is the employee who wrestles with competing desires to excel at work and to spend time at home. Mary Markey, an attorney with a prestigious national law firm, tells the story of her own psychological struggles during their Monday morning management meetings. "The group gets together to make certain that the work is being evenly distributed—to find out who needs to slack off, who can take on more. We are very busy," explains Markey. "The business just keeps coming in the door. The partners are sitting at the table, their heads in their hands, saying 'Who will do this work? We don't have enough senior people.' It is extremely difficult to sit there and be silent. Everything in me wants to say 'I can do that,'" Markey continues. "There are times a partner will say, 'Mary, maybe you can handle that.' I have to look at that person and say, 'No, I can't. Not and work part-time.' They say okay. They are truly accepting. It's me that has the hard time."

A thirty-four-year-old accountant with a Big Eight firm had this experience: "Our firm is comprised of people who are not afraid to ask you to stay late. It is an aggressive group," says Pamela Raymond, who works thirty hours a week. "They will ask. And ask, and ask once more. But, that's as far as it goes."

There are ways to communicate your schedule without jeopardizing your working relationships or the future of your flexibility. Consider these points:

❑ Be as consistent about your hours as possible.

❑ Don't be intimidated. When asked about your schedule, be friendly but firm.

❑ Ask your supervisor for support if co-workers are putting pressure on you to work extra hours.

❑ If someone plans a meeting that is not convenient for you, suggest an alternative time. If that's not possible, send a colleague in your place or request minutes from the meeting. (There will be occasions, however, when you'll want to attend meetings on your time off.)

❑ If you will be working closely on a project with a new client or someone with whom you rarely work, make sure they know your schedule from the start. That way, their expectations and your performance will be in sync.

❑ If necessary, remind co-workers that while your hours have diminished, so has your income. You may have to explain that asking you to come in on your days off is equivalent to requesting their presence on weekends.

❑ If your hours continuously exceed the agreed-upon level, negotiate with your manager for additional compensation in the form of more time off or more money.

❑ Remind *yourself* why you chose this flexible workstyle in the first place.

Create a Backup System. One surefire way to feel good about your time out of the office is knowing the bases are covered. Many flexible jobholders we interviewed told of one or more people they could rely on when they were off duty. They had support systems.

In some offices, the absence of strong backup support could mean the elimination of a flexible schedule. Chicago attorney Marie Wade credits her boss's willingness to cover for her with the success of her arrangement. Her thirty-two-hour-a-week schedule allows her to spend Fridays at home with her two children and forgo weekends in the office. "He will draft a document, participate in negotiations, or make phone calls. He does more than just put out fires," says Wade. "I keep my office very informed about the deals I'm working on so he can pick up for me if I am not around. His support distinguishes my situation from others."

Wade tells of a less fortunate attorney she knew in her firm's New York office. "We used to call each other for moral support after we had both negotiated flexible arrangements. Before long, she told me that for her part-time was 'a joke.' She wasn't getting any help in her office. Finally, she quit."

Productivity—a Measure of Success. Last year my mother-in-law, Nancy Hayes, retired after thirty years of teaching in the inner-city schools of Milwaukee. She and I have had many long conversations about the perils of raising kids and working.

She has few regrets about the years she devoted to educating Milwaukee's least fortunate children. Yet she grimaces, remembering those heartbreaking mornings when she left one of her own four children at home with the babysitter—sick. Those are the stories she tells most often. Or perhaps, those are the ones I most remember. "When your kids are sick, they are so vulnerable," she says, the last traces of guilt lingering. "It is the one time when they really want their mother. It's tough to leave them, and nearly impossible to concentrate at work."

Now she watches as the next generation of parents endures the same angst. Many of her fellow teachers are mothers with young children. "When I went into the teacher's room I'd hear them on the phone in the corner asking, 'Are you feeling better? Are you resting?' I really felt for them."

It is impossible, says Kathy Kolbe, business consultant and author of *The Conative Connection* (see Bibliography), to be productive if your mental energies are depleted by conflict. "Many people commit their mental energies to something outside of work and they just go through the motions in the office ten hours a day. If a child is sick, it is really senseless to insist that the employee stay at work. His or her mental energies are channeled toward the child."

Kolbe, a mother of two, has spent years studying how a person's motivations and innate talents affect their performance. "Most businesses have only looked at an employee's commitment to the workplace in terms of how many hours are spent on the job—not what they accomplish during those hours."

In Kolbe's view, the best way to achieve the highest level of productivity is to accept a job that fits you. "And," she says, "if that means flexible hours, so what? Employers must remember they cannot demand productivity; it must be given to them."

A person who requires structure, Kolbe advises businesses, will be most productive with set starting and quitting times. Likewise, the noncomformist will be more productive left to his or her own devices.

Most people we interviewed found that a flexible schedule provided freedom and time. Freedom to exchange days in the office for sick days home with the kids. Time to manage personal priorities: doctor appointments, errands, and activities with their children. Consequently, they returned to work refreshed and with greater focus. They believed their productivity increased.

If you can discover methods for tracking your productivity gains, you will be able to prove that flexibility is a viable workstyle for you and your company. You will also have powerful ammunition at review time. Here are some suggestions:

❑ *Set goals.* Professional firms assess productivity by tracking billable hours. Other positions lend themselves to tracking projects or individual assignments. Find a way to monitor your own output, even if it is only making it through your to-do list.

❑ *Plan ahead.* Keep a few steps ahead of yourself. Planning takes time and patience in the short term, then pays big rewards.

❑ *Avoid interruptions.* Socialization in the workplace is important, but don't go overboard. Steer clear of unnecessary conversations and activities. Stay focused.

❑ *Keep meetings short.* Make an agenda and stick to it. When you've finished the meeting get back to work.

❑ *Keep personal business to a minimum.* Reserve your off hours to handle personal calls, appointments, and family business.

MANAGING ON A FLEXIBLE SCHEDULE

Common wisdom has it that part-timers can't manage people. But, don't some of the best managers have regular travel schedules? Don't sales managers regularly supervise personnel from coast to coast? Suggesting that you must see the whites of their eyes on a daily basis is unfair to you and to your staff.

Battle for the right to retain your managerial responsibilities. Suggest a trial period. It *is* possible to be an effective manager and work a flexible schedule. (Thirty-eight percent of the professionals and managers participating in the Catalyst study on flextime were supervisors.) There will be more demands on your personal resources. But if you enjoy management, the rewards are these:

❑ A person's ability to manage people is often critical to career advancement.

❑ You will have greater visibility, more responsibility.

❑ You will have people to whom you can delegate work that you cannot fit into your schedule.

❑ Your ego will suffer less.

❑ You will reap greater satisfaction from your job.

Some flexible jobs are better suited to management than others. Too few hours in the office, or too many employees seeking your guidance, can upset the balance you are trying to achieve. Elizabeth Conway passed up a key promotion within her Los Angeles public relations firm because she knew she could not do justice to the job in shortened hours. Work four days a week, her management offered, and run the special-events division.

"I had to turn it down," says Conway, "because I knew in my heart what kind of responsibility is involved in managing fifty people. It was a young staff, which is fun. But it is tough to delegate much to inexperienced people."

Here's how, under the right circumstances, you can make a flexible managerial job work:

❑ *Provide clear direction.* Spend time with your staff going over assignments and making sure your requests are understood.

❑ *Delegate.* You don't have to do everything yourself. Pass out assignments to qualified staff.

❑ *Empower people.* Give responsibility and authority to employees who are seeking management training. You will enrich their work experience while training your successor. Thus, you will have paved the way for your own promotion.

❑ *Be available.* Your employees will be comfortable taking a turn at management if they know you are nearby, if only by phone.

❑ *Arrange for a stand-in.* If there is no one in your department ready for the training slot, ask your manager or another supervisor to fill in during a crunch.

New Orleans advertising account executive Kendall Durbin, thirty-six, found that giving employees a shot at management each week on her two days off has netted positive results. The three staff members she oversees are in their mid-twenties and relatively inexperienced. Yet Durbin has an added incentive to get them up to speed managing client assignments and projects of their own—her second child is expected any day. While she's on maternity leave, the agency management will look to Durbin's staff to keep promotions running.

"I've explained to them that my stepping out translates into potential opportunity for them," says Durbin. "It's a chance for them to prove themselves in a more visible role."

A good manager motivates and inspires. Your full-time presence is not required.

THE JOB-SHARING EXPERIENCE

While still unconventional at senior levels, job-sharing is an emerging opportunity for professionals who want to stay on track in a higher-level, full-time position. For example, a high-pressure management job that could not be handled on a three-day-a-week schedule could be shared successfully. Recent surveys indicate that approximately 16 percent of companies use job-sharing as a way to provide more flexibility.

This is how it works: Most pairs jointly take on a full-time position; they are equally responsible for the full range of the job. In other cases, they take on different aspects of the job. While they have separate assignments, the partners cover for each other. Occasionally, job-sharing is used to describe two people in unrelated positions, paired only for headcount purposes.

As a job-sharer you will provide your employer several benefits:

❑ *Reduced absenteeism.* Job-sharers often cover for each other for reasons ranging from parental leave to a dentist appointment.

❑ *Improved scheduling.* Peak times and heavy work loads can be covered by both members of the team when necessary. Or, if the job calls for two employees to be in different places at the same time, job-sharers can handle it.

❑ *Double input.* A job-sharing pair brings two sets of skills, experiences, and viewpoints to the table.

❑ *Greater continuity.* If one partner leaves or is gone for an extended period of time, the other is available to train and bring on board a new teammate. In certain cases, the remaining partner can cover the entire job until a replacement is found.

❑ *Training opportunities.* One partner has the opportunity to learn from the other. In some cases a junior/senior team can work when the intent is to train and bring on board a person to fill the more experienced person's shoes.

HOW YOU CAN BENEFIT FROM JOB-SHARING

Choose the Right Partner. When Susan and I began our job-sharing arrangement, we were easily able to carve out portions of the job that best suited our individual talents. As codirectors of marketing communications, she would handle speechwriting and the publications and I would take on publicity and promotions. Because we both had held the full-time position and worked together before, our match made sense.

Choosing the right partner is the most important and potentially most complex component of ensuring success for your job-sharing arrangement. To effectively share a position, both parties must discuss detail. How will you handle people, assignments, pressure, communications, and scheduling? How will you be held accountable?

A job-sharing arrangement often results in an integration of professional and personal lives. Throughout our interviews it was often compared to a marriage. "I never thought it would be like this," comments Sarah Goldsborough, twenty-nine, who shares a graphic arts position in Minneapolis with another working mother. "We end up talking so much together about our work, people, and our attitudes that the relationship has really intensified. We have a lot in common."

It is difficult to determine just what will make a partnership click. Often it is the subtle differences that can make or break an arrangement. Still, the best job-sharing partners are those who:

❑ *Have the same philosophy of work.* You agree on how you will accomplish the requirements of the job.

❑ *Are friends, but not best friends.* The most successful pairs seem to have mutual respect for one another personally and professionally. However, it's considered unwise to mix too much personal time with professional time.

❑ *Share a similar style.* While job-sharers need not be clones of one another, similarities in style are helpful. If one person rebels against structured work and the other only feels comfortable presenting picture-perfect reports, there is a potential for conflict. Such a combination might work beautifully until the two are expected to present a common approach.

❑ *Have complementary skills and training.* In combination, you should bring a full range of knowledge and talent to the position.

❑ *Have similar expectations for the arrangement.* Your personal agendas will dictate the way the work is handled and presented. If one partner is aiming for the president's chair and the other is content with the status quo, discontentment could arise.

❏ *Are not overly competitive.* A little competition is healthy. But to be effective, a job-sharing duo must work as a cohesive unit, supporting one another's efforts.

❏ *Are honest with one another.* You must be direct and communicate constantly. If a problem arises, resolve it swiftly.

Molly Lange, a thirty-six-year-old staff attorney for a U.S. government agency, was forced to examine the intricacies of her job-sharing arrangement when her partner, Barbara Black, thirty-five, announced she was leaving.

"When she first told me I felt like my husband was moving out on me," recalls Lange. "After I got used to the idea I was able to say, 'I will miss you. You must do what's right for you.' "

Four years ago, Lange and Black put together a job-sharing proposal. They had worked together in the same department for several years. They trusted one another's instincts. So did their boss; he approved the proposal.

Their reasons for wanting to scale back were different: Lange has two children and was finding the management of a legal career and family too exhausting. Black wanted time off to write mystery novels.

Now, with Black's departure approaching, Lange is looking for a new partner. She believes it will be hard to improve on the situation she has had. The search process, however, has included the examination of what was good and not so good about her partnership with Black.

"We complemented each other very well," says Lange. "I loved to go to meetings; she hated meetings. Often we were able to adjust our duties along the lines of what we like to do. People could sense our differences and some would work with one of us better than the other."

Lange and Black are friends but rarely socialize outside of the office. Their lifestyles are different. But in the course of their job-share, staying in touch was easy, leaving notes on the computer and talking on the phone. "It usually worked better to talk on Barbara's day at home, because my personal life is busier than hers. It was easy because we actually liked talking to one another."

Near the top of the positive column for Lange was the fact that she and Black shared similar views. "We have very similar attitudes about the powers that be and the issues we work on," Lange explains. "Barbara and I think the same people and things are ridiculous. When you are looking for a new partner you can't exactly go out and poll people on issues like that."

If there was a down side to their partnership, it was a break in enthusiasm about taking on more work. "When we were given an assignment, I would always want to please the boss. I wanted the strokes," explains Lange. "Sometimes, Barbara would tell the boss, 'No, you ask too much of me.' " Lange will look for a new teammate who is interested in eventually applying for a more challenging job together.

Agreeing to job-share means you have enough confidence in yourself to share every aspect of your work with another person. "In a way, this new match-up will be a test of my ego," says Lange. "What if this person overshadows me? The person you share your job with knows everything about the work you do. There are no secrets."

WORKING OUT THE DETAILS WHEN YOU SHARE A JOB

All decisions about how your new job will work must be made in tandem with your partner. Here are a few of the things you must consider:

Covering for One Another. Most jobs are split fifty-fifty. Will you have any overlap time for staff meetings or to review commitments? Will you fill in for one another for long or short intervals? It is far better to decide these questions ahead of time. You'll avoid misunderstandings with your supervisor and co-workers. If you increase hours to cover, will you be compensated?

Working with Clients. Ensure that your clients receive an equal if not better level of service than they would get if they worked with one person. Will you split the client group or manage them together? Special attention to detail and communication strategies will keep you on track with your clients.

Good Communication Is a Key. As in any good union, effective communication is critical to the success of a job-sharing arrangement. Most job-sharers communicate by phone. Some meet regularly for breakfast or lunch. Others leave messages on computers and voice mail. Find the approach that works best for you.

Working with Your Supervisor. To the extent possible, you and your partner will want to present a united front to your supervisor. It will be important to prove that you work well as a team. Agree beforehand on the content and an approach when making a presentation to your manager.

Judgment Day. While most job-sharers split their responsibilities and a salary down the middle, they are generally reviewed by management separately. You and your partner will want to prepare for your review together to cast the most positive light on your work arrangement.

If One Partner Leaves. Job-sharing has little history upon which to draw. We suggest, however, that if your partner moves on, take the opportunity to reevaluate your work options. If you like sharing a job, find another partner. You can draw on your experience to locate the right person. On the other hand, the timing may be right to consider a return to full-time work or shortened hours.

CAN JOB-SHARERS MANAGE?

Can job-sharers manage? The short answer: yes. Many of the same benefits job-sharers offer to their employer are available to subordinates. For example, a subordinate's work experience will be enriched, drawing from the experience, education, and training of two individuals.

Pat Quinn Casper, who shares the management job of pediatric hospice coordinator with Hanneke Deeken, compares the role of job-sharer as manager to that of a parent. "My husband and I use the same team approach with our children. Hanneke and I won't take a stand on a major issue with an employee until we've discussed it," says Casper. "If it is a discipline problem we talk about it, and then present our position as one."

Other guidelines for effective management include:

❑ Many management decisions require on-the-spot action. Decide whether or not the person on the job will have full responsibility for those judgment calls.

❑ On major issues, make it clear to subordinates that the decision for action was reached together.

❑ Be consistent.

❑ If you do have differences in management philosophies, work them out. Avoid confusing your staff.

❑ When decisions or actions are taken in the absence of the other, be sure the details are communicated swiftly. You won't want to ambush your partner.

❑ Never undermine your partner by questioning a management decision in front of your staff.

THE TELECOMMUTING EXPERIENCE

Advances in technology have made it easier than ever to telecommute. Now you can communicate instantly with your workplace, whether it is down the street or around the globe. Today's home office can be a virtual replica of the one in the office tower—complete with all the right gear—fax, phone, computer, and modem.

Even though the tools are there to get the job done, some employers are still uneasy if they can't see your face. Yet, if you are telecommuting, you are in substantial company; nearly 15 million people work at home full- or part-time.

For the most part, employers who've tried telecommuting or work at home like it. Here's why:

❑ *Cost savings.* The rising cost of office space, particularly in major markets, is a major expense item for employers. The additional costs associated with building management—insurance, security, and parking, for example—also are reduced. In Colorado, lack of space launched both the U S West's and the city of Boulder's telecommuting programs.

❑ *Increased productivity.* Telecommuting enables you to work when you work best, which may not always coincide with traditional work hours. With fewer distractions, employees can focus on the task at hand, rather than being pulled into company banter. One U S West telecommuter reports his productivity jumped 50 percent after he left the office.

❑ *Improved morale.* If home is where you'd rather be, your attitude toward work will improve.

❑ *Extended service.* Customer service agents, information processors, and sales representatives have a competitive advantage if they are able to expand their hours beyond the traditional hours of service.

WORKING OUT THE DETAILS OF TELECOMMUTING

Space. If you are going to telecommute, find a space within your home that is quiet and suitable for your work. If you will need technical backup—a computer, modem, printer, or copying machine—will it fit in the space you've set aside? Are the necessary energy sources present? Some companies will even want to approve your work space before the telecommuting arrangement is approved.

Time. One of the advantages of working at home is that you can choose the time when you work best. It is advisable that you try to stick to some routine. That way colleagues will be able to reach you easily. Your children will become accustomed to the times you are available for play.

Help. Anyone who has tried to get by without help knows you will need child care if you plan to work at home. You will, however, have more opportunity to visit with your children during the day. Most telecommuting parents we interviewed took time out for lunch, snacks, or an after-school chat with their kids. And, should an emergency arise, you are there to handle it.

Face-to-face. Most companies require that the telecommuter spend time in the office to stay in touch with the business and to avoid isolation. For the parents we spoke with, any feelings of isolation were more than offset by the chance to spend extra hours with their family. Still, there are benefits to visiting at least once a week with your supervisor and colleagues. Just under the surface, the attitude often lingers that an employee must be seen to be appreciated. Come review and promotion time, you want your face to be familiar.

Tools of Communication. The more you are out of the office, the more important it will be for you to have an effective means of communicating with your office. Fax machines, computers and modems, couriers, and, of course, the telephone are tools you can use to stay in touch.

UP THE LADDER

In our conversations with flexible jobholders, the subject of promotability inevitably came up. Initially the discussion stirred up talk of the Mommy Track and stalled careers. But often the conversation turned to their choice: less time in the office, less travel, fewer clients, less pressure, fewer demands. It wasn't that these parents were opposed to advancement. It was this: they had opted for a better balance between work and family. As a result, they didn't expect rapid promotions or partnership.

Liza Handy, a lawyer and mother working thirty hours a week in Chicago, is one example. Says Handy: "I just don't think about partnership anymore. I have my immediate priorities. Maybe when I finish my child-rearing years I will reevaluate. But, right now it is not important to me."

For those who want to stay in motion, promotion from the part-time ranks is possible.

Jennifer Dials moved from three days on special projects to a four-day position managing advertising for a large utility company.

Ann Conover was promoted from a three-day-a-week public relations job to a vice-president's slot requiring four days in the office. She's in the insurance industry.

At one of the nation's most prestigious law firms, Madeline Bollinger turned her back on the partnership track but was still promoted a notch above associate. She works thirty-five hours a week.

Within the best companies, human resources professionals vow to push flexible job holders up the ladder.

Meanwhile, others, like job-sharers Ann Saliers and Peggy Hoogerhyde at Steelcase, eagerly pursue promotion. They entered their arrangement knowing other job-sharers within their company had been rewarded for achievement.

Typically, at the time a flexible arrangement was negotiated, most parents were so grateful for a breather they didn't focus on their prospects for promotion. If you need a break from the fast lane, take it. But don't wait for your supervisor to bring up the subject of your career advancement. He or she may take your flexible schedule and failure to address the issue as signals you've scaled back for good. It you want to move ahead, make your intentions known.

Here's what you can do:

❏ *Talk to your boss.* At the earliest opportunity, talk to your manager about prospects for promotion. Will you be eligible? To the extent that *you* can, fill him or her in on your future career goals. For example, do you plan to return to work full-time when your children are in school?

❏ *Ask for substantive work.* Julie Evert, a project manager in a San Diego real estate development office, found that all the loose ends were saved for her three days in the office. Don't let that happen to you. If you find that the best projects aren't being handed to you, ask for them.

❏ *Prove that you are still ambitious.* Take the initiative on projects, speak up at meetings, and offer creative solutions to departmental problems. Offer to take on a particularly difficult task that can be handled within the time constraints of your position.

❏ *Share your ideas.* One advertising executive on a three-day-a-week schedule remarked that her employer treated her as though her "brain stopped working on Tuesdays and Thursdays." Share those ideas that spring forth at the park with your children. Prove to your management that your creative juices or problem-solving powers still flow outside of office hours.

❏ *Go the extra mile.* Without jeopardizing your flexible arrangement, volunteer for a special task force, put in a few extra hours. Be enthusiastic. Your efforts will symbolize your commitment to your job and your organization.

❏ *Document your successes.* Keep track of your work and be prepared to make your case for promotion when review time comes.

10

THINGS YOU SHOULD KNOW ABOUT JOB FLEXIBILITY

On the sun-drenched University of California, Berkeley, campus, author Arlie Hochschild teaches a class called Sociology of Gender. Her students are mostly young women, a different breed from those who stormed in rebellion on the campus squares there and elsewhere a quarter-century ago. They are optimistic about their future; they envision an interesting career, two or three children, a fulfilling marriage, perhaps a station wagon and a white picket fence.

In her book *The Second Shift,* Hochschild describes her students' unwillingness to face up to the real-life problems of managing a demanding career and family. "These are intelligent, inquiring women. I think they are avoiding a close look because it scares them," she writes.

It is Hochschild's concern that this whole generation of young women is ignoring what needs to happen to make their lives as career people and parents whole. So for her part, she has written *The Second Shift,* detailing the struggle women undertake to complete two jobs—one for pay, the other at home. She also tries to paint a clear picture in the classroom. "Arlie talks for weeks about gloom and doom and then she calls me in as the ray of hope," says Linda Marks. A consultant and lecturer, Marks talks to the students about flexible jobs. It is, she tells them, their opportunity to balance work and family.

For the parent who puts in a full day at the office, then goes home to work the second shift, finding flexibility in the workplace is more than a ray of hope; it is a virtual rainbow on the horizon.

In this final chapter we pass along the impressions, emotions, and reactions—negative and positive—of the parents with whom we spoke. For them flexibility is, or will soon become, a way of life.

THE ECONOMICS OF FLEXIBILITY.

About halfway through my work on this book, my friends Hannah and Peter Burlington came to visit me. They were expecting their first child. Throughout their three-day visit, they shared plans for their new family: they would, of course, need a bigger house, a yard, room for a swing set—oh, and a station wagon. Where *do* you vacation with children?

Many conversations passed before we discussed the component of their lives that had postponed this visit for three years: their careers. Hannah is a pediatric medical evacuation nurse. She works long hours, is on night call, and goes days without sleep. Peter is a trial attorney with a bustling practice. He works seven days a week.

My concern for them was twofold. First, there wasn't much room in their current lives for each other, let alone for a baby.

Second, I saw them falling into a baby-boomer trap: starting a family and buying a bigger house and a new car. *They were leveraging themselves out of full-time parenthood, eliminating the choice.*

To avoid drowning in debt's high waters, many fast-track, two-income families need just that: two incomes to handle elephant-sized mortgages, payments on imported cars, travel. That means parents like Hannah Burlington can't afford to scale back a full-time job to be with their children.

There are ways to avoid economic pain if you want career flexibility:

❑ *Plan ahead.* Delay the trappings of success until after you have decided how you and your family will balance work and family.

❑ *Reshape your schedule.* Opt for telecommuting, work at home, or compressed work weeks if you want to reduce the pressure but keep the full-time salary.

❑ *Be realistic.* Financial strain can cause just as much stress to a family as two brutal schedules. Before you take a cut in pay and hours make sure your bank account can handle it. A reporter for a big-city daily newspaper pulled strings to get the publisher's approval for a job-share. To her embarrassment, she had to pass on the opportunity. She couldn't afford it.

Kate Conover had a happier experience. She went from working full-time to sharing a vice-president's job in a Jacksonville bank. Before she accepted the position, Conover wanted to know what her net monthly loss would be. Because her baby-sitter actually wanted to cut back too, Conover was able to save considerably on child care. When she determined she would only have a net loss of $200 in income, she and her husband determined it was workable. To save further, they agreed to cut both their maid and lawn service.

Many parents make the extra effort to stretch financial resources, considering the benefits of flexibility to be far more valuable than the extras (dinners out, nails done, weekends away) they do without.

Doing Double Duty. "I was the envy of the women in my neighborhood," says Barbara Morazza. "They saw my husband driving car pools, going to the grocery store. Well, it all came to a screeching halt when I cut back my hours. Suddenly he thought he had a *wife*."

Morazza's experience is not uncommon. Husbands who shelled out at least some measure of assistance when their wives were working full-time reverted to a vision of yesteryear when they saw a break in the nineties routine.

"I couldn't believe it," said another woman who had shortened her hours. "During my first week on the new schedule my husband handed me a wad of dirty shirts and said, 'Would you mind dropping these off at the cleaners? Medium starch.' For the past three years he had been dropping them off himself on the way to the office. I was so stunned, I did it. That was my mistake."

Part of the problem is this: while working full-time, women had little time to cook, organize closets, or arrange special activities for their children. A number of women told us that their first reaction was to make up for lost time around the house. They baked cookies, prepared fancy meals, hung wallpaper. Their husbands observed and fell into what they hoped was a new routine.

Further, to afford less time on the job, parents cut back on household help. Rarely is the leftover housework then shared by both spouses. "My husband always expected me to take responsibility for the house," reported a thirty-eight-year-old part-time law librarian. "When I worked full-time he knew it was hard to fit everything in. But with two days off, I can hear him thinking, 'Now what's your problem?' It wouldn't occur to him to help."

We heard women express this concern: Will trading off hours at work for more work at home eliminate the strides woman have made? "There are side effects to negotiating these work schedules," says Kathleen Christensen, author of *Women and Home-based Work*. "The woman starts doing much of the housework she spent a long time negotiating away."

If you sense the power balance shifting at home, address

the issue at once. Don't let the time you've created to be with your family be eaten up by extra housework.

The Myth About Child Care. Parents fantasize about eliminating child care. Child care is very expensive, time-con-suming in its own way, and, as one mother put it, "It is rarely custom-designed for our own children." But, the facts are these:

1) If you're a telecommuter, you must have someone taking care of the kids. One mother of three young children, who writes for a magazine from home, told us this story: "My baby-sitter called in sick. Rather than go through the hassle of finding a substitute, I thought I could make it through one day on my own. I should have known better. It was a series of small disasters capped off by this: my middle son walked into my computer room while I was changing the baby's diaper. Some-how, within minutes, he wiped out everything. It took me a month to get my computer repaired. The repair service was never quite able to tell me just what he'd done. I'll never even attempt working like that again."

Another telecommuting mother tried to eliminate child care altogether. Understandably, she couldn't get her work done during the day because of the demands of motherhood. "I ended up working in the middle of the night," she recalls. "That didn't last long. I was completely exhausted."

2) If your child-care provider is flexible, you will be able to cut down on the cost. A good number of part-time profes-sionals, however, found they needed reliable backup care so they could work if they had to.

3) Some parents reported difficulty finding part-time care for their kids. Particularly in areas where competition for the best care is stiff, providers were hesitant to take children for less than full-time. If they could afford it, parents preferred com-mitting to full-time care rather than sacrificing quality.

Who Could Have Known? Many women who find themselves in the work/family pickle are tenacious and achieve-ment-oriented. They have worked hard, fast, and long to reach the top—to have it all. And now they say incredulously, This isn't going to work! They recognize they will not be partner, president, CEO.

They are resentful. "I truly believed I would be able to do it all," said one mother of three, who has given up a shot at a law firm partnership to spend more time with her kids. "I mean, why not? I had always excelled at everything else."

To say they've resigned themselves to working less makes these women sound querulous. Rather, they have opted for scaled-back careers because they care more about their families than about their work. They also witness the price paid by women who made other choices: infertility, divorce, loneliness.

Portland attorney June Henderson, thirty-eight, passed on partnership in order to spend more time with her kids. She has this to say: "It isn't that easy at my level of seniority to watch younger people move ahead of me. People don't make me feel like a second-class citizen, but sometimes I do. I basically resolve it by looking at my family; they are my priority now. Even looking to the future, I ask myself, At what point will these four children not need a big piece of my life? I think it will be a very long time."

Never ones to give up easily, these achievers have worked out alternatives: they job-share, telecommute, shorten their hours, or compress their week. Still, they say, it's not the same. It's not like being on top of the heap. But it's for a good cause.

Perception as Reality. Regardless of their true commitment to work, some parents felt that once they scaled back their hours, they were treated differently by management. But they didn't just sit there and take it. They demanded more interesting work and reminded their colleagues of their credentials and commitment. And if they didn't get the respect they deserved, they sent the ultimate message: they quit.

Creeping Commitment. These innovators, gutsy enough to negotiate this front line of flexibility, were the same overachievers once committed to power hours. With another victory under their belts, the challenge for them was to scale back, relax. "It was very, very hard for me to set limits for myself in the office," explains Wendy Blake, a thirty-three-year-old employee relations manager in Houston. "I was so accustomed to running things, to being involved in every project. Letting go to someone else happened slowly."

These employees had risen to company stardom by saying yes to every management request. Their tendency was always to exceed and excel. Now, with some of the traditional external cues missing—late nights, weekends in the office—they still had to prove they were serious about their work. What happened?

FLEXIBLE JOBS: TEN PITFALLS TO AVOID

1. Don't let your eagerness to work less sap your negotiating strength. Remember you are a valuable asset.

2. Reducing your work schedule will likely reduce your income. Be sure you can afford to work part-time before you negotiate for change.

3. Some Type-A individuals have difficulty cutting back their work load. Avoid creeping commitment. Don't be one who puts in forty hours and is compensated for twenty.

4. Make sure the hours you've agreed to work match the requirements of the job. Too much responsibility will only lead to frustration for all.

5. Beware of a shift in the power balance at home. Keep the lines of communication open. Don't replace office work with housework.

6. Don't expect to accomplish much work at home without the appropriate child-care arrangements.

7. If you get all your strokes from your job, prepare for some ego adjustments. Important things *will* happen on a day when you're working at home.

8. Some supervisors save the uninteresting work for the "part-time crew." If the content of your work is not up to par, discuss it with your boss.

9. The relationship between job-sharers has often been compared to a marriage. Make sure you and your job-share partner are compatible and are both good communicators.

10. Some colleagues may assume that your part-time schedule signals a lack of commitment to the job. Do your best to exude the same confidence and professionalism that won your employer's support.

They were working far too many hours and getting paid far too little. They had to learn to give up some control and stop trying to get more.

THE GOOD NEWS ABOUT FLEXIBLE JOBS

Time. The scarcest resource of all is time. It is what these people were looking for, and for the most part they found it. They wanted time with their families for simple things: a picnic in the park, reading bedtime stories, leisurely lunch together. Time to lie in the grass and watch the clouds float by. These were moments they didn't want to miss.

Sometimes those moments came none too soon.

Not unlike other full-time working mothers, Abby Parker, thirty-four, did everything she could to fit in extra moments with her three children. A demanding schedule as a federal lobbyist for an environmental group made it difficult. She had proposed scaling back her duties and hours. She wanted to work for three days only. She needed the free time for her children.

On this day, she awaits the verdict. Lunchtime, she is picking up her son at preschool. As usual, she is in a hurry. This is what happens: "Walking from the school to our car, we pass the playground," explains Parker. "Lots of times, the other moms are out there watching their kids, swinging and climbing. I always look at them with envy. Thomas does too. He always asks, 'Can we stop?' I always say, 'No, not today, some other time,' and hurry him along."

Today her son starts to cry. This is not a tantrum. It is genuine, deep disappointment, frustration. Dollops of tears fall from his round face. "Every day you say 'not today,' " says the boy. "There never is 'some other time.' "

"I realize he is right," says Parker. "I pray my new schedule will be approved."

It is. After school on her next free day, mother and son stop at the park.

How did flexibility make a difference? Beyond life's pleasurable moments, parents want time for practical things. They don't want their lives to depend on the all-night grocery store, the toy shop that delivers birthday presents, personal shoppers, or same-day cleaners. Said one mother on a flexible schedule: "I won't ever have to be up past midnight sewing a school costume again."

Less Stress. According to a 1988 Bureau of National Affairs study, the number one health risk for working women is stress. Not surprisingly, the leading cause of that stress is balancing work and family.

Full-time working mothers become so adept at managing the myriad details that often they don't realize the pressures they are under. In Hartford, the doctor told thirty-year-old Julieanne Buxton that the cause of her chronic stomach problems was probably stress, too many commitments. She didn't believe him. "I'm used to running like this," she told him. After four months of repeated problems she sought a second opinion. Without waiting for the test results, the second doctor suggested this: perhaps managing a full-time job, travel, two children, a husband, and a household was the cause of her aches

---

FLEXIBLE JOBS: TEN PAYOFFS YOU CAN EXPECT

1. More time to bond with a newborn
2. More time for your children
3. More time to spend with your spouse
4. More organization, reduced stress
5. More time for yourself—to exercise, read, or do nothing
6. More time to devote to your community or your child's school
7. More time to pursue new interests and friendships
8. A chance to keep your career on track without sacrificing too much time with family
9. The potential for savings from reduced child-care costs and commuting
10. A greater sense of balance and well-being

and pains. "Not possible," Buxton insisted. After six more months, she began to think perhaps the doctors had been right. She decided to cut back at work. Her plan for a three-day work week was approved just before the start of a two-week family vacation. Before she returned her health problems had subsided.

A flexible schedule reduces some of the pressure and a lot of the guilt, parents reported. "I'm embarrassed to say this," confides one mother on a shortened schedule, "but there were times when the decision of whether or not to take my child to the doctor was heavily influenced by what was happening in the office. That doesn't happen any more, and I can barely admit that at one point it did."

With fewer professional commitments, parents have more time to attend to their physical as well as their psychological health. They are exercising more and simply feeling better.

Neighborhood, School, Community. Within a few weeks of paring my own schedule down to three days, I got a phone call from Bianca Beary, head room mother for my son's first-grade class. She was calling to inform me of my duties as assistant room mother. Before I had a chance to tell her that I had a job, there must be some mistake; I couldn't volunteer, I couldn't commit, they'd be happier with someone else, she had finished her speech and congratulated me on my new assignment. Clearly, Bianca Beary wouldn't take no for an answer. After I realized I *did* have time to be a school volunteer and they didn't need my management skills to run the first grade, it worked out well. I was able to relax and get to know some remarkable women and their children.

Other parents reported similar experiences. For the first time, they were able to take their turn in the car pools, volunteer for school activities, attend the block party, drive for field trips and to afternoon sports practices.

One mother landed a part in community theater and recruited her children to work on the crew. Another was able to take her turn at the co-op nursery school, still another choreographed the grade-school musical.

Improved Relationships. When time is tight and the

pressure is on, the people you care most about sometimes get the least attention.

Your Family. Families take time: birthday parties, holidays, hearing about your sister's boyfriend, your cousin's new baby. With less time at work, at least now there is room for family.

"I Federal Expressed my mother's birthday present every year," recalls thirty-six-year-old Melissa Rose, of her days as a full-time attorney in Denver. "Back then, she fared better than most: she actually got something. Now I have time to give some thought to her gift and send it by regular mail."

Your Spouse. A husband and wife managing kids and two full-time careers work hard to fit in all the necessities. Then, if there is time left over (and there rarely is), they can squeeze in time for each other. Usually, by then, they are too tired to talk. However, with some time off from work, there is more energy to go around.

"Our life is still very busy," reports Ann Mason, who cut her Kansas City interior design business back to four days a week. "But every now and then we meet after work for a glass of wine, or we have a late dinner once the children are in bed. Before, I never even had time to think of those things, let alone plan them."

In an era when barely half of all marriages endure, couples need time to stay in touch just to have a chance at maintaining their relationship. Parents spending less time at work told us this: they were finally taking evenings, weekends, or vacations away with their spouse. "We wouldn't have considered it before I cut back my hours," says working mother Mary Ann Maxwell. "We spent all our free time with the kids. We felt we had to." They reported more conversation, more shared interests, more quiet time together.

Your Friends. In decades past, moms gathered around the kitchen table, cups in hand, sharing secrets about their lives. When I was in my twenties, I used to tease my own mother about her outings with the "gals" or my memories of her bridge club. She never really said much. Now I know why. She and her friends had one up on the single-minded, career-focused women of the eighties and nineties.

Marcy Graham, a thirty-six-year-old television news reporter in Baltimore, tells this story: "When my mother saw I was stressed out, she would tell me, 'Go have lunch with a friend.' 'Friends?' I would ask. 'What friends? All I ever do is work.' " Now, she says, "What my two days off have given me is time to get to know some other mothers. It's added another dimension to my life."

Having friends to share the challenges of mixing work with parenthood relieves some of the strain, we were told repeatedly by those we surveyed.

Keeping Your Foot in the Door. Jane Philips grew up in an affluent suburb outside New York City. She attended the right schools along with the daughters of her parents' successful friends. She recently returned from her high school reunion, perplexed. "I really expected all these bright young women to be doing all kinds of interesting work," says Philips, thirty-seven. "Very few of them were working at all because they had kids. It seems like such a waste of talent."

Phillips is grateful that her four-day-a-week association management position keeps her in the professional loop. "My sister is a physician," says Philips. "She took off when her children were small. Now, in her mid-thirties, she is starting again from the bottom."

Particularly for those who know that someday they want to go back to working full-time, keeping skills sharpened through a flexible job is important. "Our industry changes so quickly," said Colorado engineer Colleen Clark, "that if I couldn't stay in touch by telecommuting, it would be very difficult to catch up later."

Time for a Special Relationship. We asked in Part I, "How much time is enough time? How much time does a mother need with her baby; a baby with its mother?" Parental leaves aside, the answer seems to be that a flexible job allows you to ease gently back into the workplace. It eliminates that dramatic full-time break between mother and child.

In talking with women in the course of our research, we were told how much they wanted to spend those first months with their child. "I didn't want to hear about that first step from my baby-sitter," said one mother. "I wanted to see it with my own eyes." They wanted it badly enough, in some cases, to risk losing their jobs by proposing a flexible job. Most of them said that if it hadn't gone their way they wouldn't have returned to work at all.

In March of 1989, my third son was born nine weeks early. He was hospitalized and critically ill for nearly three months. Had I not been granted a six-month maternity leave and a part-time return to work, I would have had only one option: to quit. My phase-in to work was good not only for me and my baby, but for my company. The first year after his birth, I visited a hospital or pediatrician almost every week, sometimes more; sometimes carting in all three boys when winter dealt her annual bouts of flu. Had my schedule not been flexible, I surely would have nipped at company time. As it was, I think they hardly noticed the extreme demands of my children.

The first year of your child's life is special; he or she transforms from a tiny bundle, dependent on you to fulfill every need, to a bundle of energy, climbing and communicating, exhibiting early signs of eventual independence.

The parents we spoke with didn't want to miss any more than they had to. "Our nanny was terrific, everything was going fine," recalls San Franciscan Jane Easton of the decision to cut her hours in half. "But it was Christmastime and he was becoming so animated. I wanted to be there."

Flexible jobs have provided Easton, and parents like her, with the chance to be as much a part of their child's early life as possible. If there is such a thing as having it all, those we interviewed said combining family and flexible work is it.

PART

III

RESOURCES
FOR YOUR
JOB SEARCH

CORPORATE
POLICY
GUIDE

TWENTY-FIVE FLEXIBLE FIRMS

These twenty-five companies have some of the most progressive flexible work policies in American industry. This list is not intended as a "top twenty-five." Instead, we've tried to provide a sampling of some of the best, most innovative, and most widely used programs.

In compiling this list, we reviewed data on more than 150 companies with at least 5,000 employees and contacted more than fifty of the most flexible companies, looking for answers to some of these questions: Are people who work fewer than thirty-five hours a week eligible for benefits? Is job-sharing, work-from-home, and part-time work an option throughout the organization? Has the company taken steps to encourage flexibility? Is an unpaid parental leave available as well as the option of a part-time return following maternity leave? And, what other work-family programs are in place?

Unless otherwise noted, all of these companies have a standard paid disability leave for pregnant women, generally ranging from six to eight weeks. In almost every case, the flexible options described are bestowed at a supervisor's discretion. In other words, if you work for one of these companies and your supervisor has not gotten with the program, or if your job is not suited to flexible conditions, there's no guarantee that flexibility will be an option.

> Aetna Life & Casualty Co.
> 151 Farmington Avenue
> Hartford, Connecticut 06156
> 203-273-0123

Companies that actually promote flexibility are few and far between, but Aetna is one of them. The company posts openings for job-shares and publishes guidelines for employees and supervisors on alternative schedules. Aetna has changed its headcount policies to open the way for more flexibility (a half-timer now counts as a half-person) and encourages managers to review every job opening to determine whether in fact it could be done in less time. A full-time consultant on family issues helps facilitate negotiations for flexible jobs.

The company's formal, company-wide programs include staggered hours, flextime (core hours nine to three), job-sharing, and part-time schedules. Part-timers who work fifteen or more hours a week are eligible for full benefits. A family-leave policy, introduced in 1988, allows up to six months unpaid leave for family care with a job guarantee. Supervisors have the option of granting additional time, as well as a part-time arrangement for returning mothers. According to Shèrry Herchenroether, manager of family services, before the new policy went into effect, Aetna was losing women during the year following their maternity leaves. Now, although women are taking an average of five weeks' additional of unpaid leave following their disability leave, they're staying with the company.

Other work/family benefits include: paid time off to care for a sick family member; a referral service for child care and eldercare; a pretax salary set-aside for dependent care; and funding for training of day-care providers. Personal days are left to the supervisor's discretion.

> American Express
> 200 Vesey Street
> World Financial Center
> New York, New York 10285
> 212-640-2000

American Express, one of the first companies to explore child-care resources and referral, allows flextime, job-sharing, and part-time work in some of its business units. A pilot telecommuting program was under way in 1990. Since 1989, the company has introduced a number of programs that support flexibility. Among them: part-timers who work a minimum of fourteen hours a week can buy into full-time benefits and are eligible for the company's family-leave program and prorated adoption assistance.

Following a 1989 survey, when employees expressed a need for more flexibility, company executives issued a series of letters encouraging their operating divisions to develop some flexible options. Rennie Roberts, senior vice-president of human resources for the corporation, maintains that the big push for flexibility has only just begun; she expects initiatives to bubble up from individual operating groups and divisions in the years ahead.

The company's family-leave program allows for a full-time leave of up to twelve weeks (including standard medical disability leave) and a gradual part-time return on prorated salary. Total leave time allowed, combining the full-time and part-time absence, is twenty weeks. Fathers and adoptive parents are also eligible.

As of January 1, 1990, the number of personal days was increased from four to five per year for full-time employees (prorated for part-timers); employees may take that time on a half-day or emergency basis without prior scheduling.

American Express supports local child-care initiatives—the company budgeted $800,000 for that purpose in 1989—and introduced a child-care subsidy in January 1991. Some business units offer nationwide child-care resources and referral services. Policies vary by business unit.

The Arthur Andersen Worldwide Organization
69 West Washington Street
Chicago, Illinois 60602
312-580-0069

Arthur Andersen and Andersen Consulting, the U.S. member firms of The Arthur Andersen Worldwide Organization, which provides audit, business advisory, tax, and corporate specialty services and information technology consulting, have a history of leadership in the work/family arena. The company's Flexible Work Program for Managers allows new mothers returning from leave to work part-time for up to three years. Although designed to accommodate professionals, who generally reach manager level between the ages of twenty-seven and twenty-nine, other employees have been known to take advantage of the program. Benefits, reviews, and salary adjustments for participating partner-track managers remain in place, but the timing of promotions is slowed. Peter Pesce, managing director of human resources for the firm, expects the program to open the way for more flexibility in other job categories. As of 1990, about forty U.S. offices have experimented with the program and about a hundred managers have participated.

Arthur Andersen has an unusually generous maternity leave plan. After three years of service, employees are eligible for up to ninety days paid disability leave. All employees have the option of taking an unpaid parental leave that may last up to one year. Other work/family supports include adoption aid of up to $2,500, nationwide referral for day care and eldercare, and a pretax salary set-aside for dependent care.

Bausch & Lomb
One Lincoln First Square
Rochester, New York 14601-0054
716-338-6000

At Bausch & Lomb, the international healthcare and optics company, a request for flexibility can't be denied unless it has been "thoroughly reviewed" by the human resources department. In other words, a supervisor does not have the power to summarily reject a request for shorter hours or revised starting and quitting times. The company's commitment to flexibility extends beyond headquarters. Manufacturing sites are encouraged to adopt flexibility whenever possible. Bausch & Lomb, which has "two or three dozen people sharing jobs," posts job-shares internally and, when necessary, advertises outside the company to fill job-share openings. Benefits are prorated for part-timers, provided an employee works a minimum of seventeen and a half hours a week.

The company's child-care leave policy allows for twelve weeks leave, but, according to D. Donald Errigo, director of employee relations for the corporation, if an employee needs more time, leaves can be extended. Right now, Bausch & Lomb has an "occasional absence" policy—up to five days' worth of time—from which employees can draw in hourly or daily increments for emergency, paid time off. As of 1990, the company is in the process of reviewing its time-off policies to give employees more flexibility in how they choose to use vacation days, holidays, and sick days. Other work/family policies include child-care and eldercare referral.

Corning
Corning Glass Works
Houghton Park
Corning, New York 14831
607-974-9000

In 1986, when Corning started looking at work/family policies, women were leaving the company at twice the rate of white males. In 1987, the

New York State–based firm, which competes in the fields of specialty materials, consumer housewares, laboratory sciences, and telecommunications, launched a part-time work policy. It encourages job-sharing, work-from-home, and part-time options for salaried employees. Since then, Corning has documented the fact that more high-potential women are staying with the company. The company has published a work/family kit that outlines the part-time policy and related programs and benefits for salaried employees and their supervisors. At this writing, about forty of the 6,000 eligible salaried employees were on some form of alternative schedule. Of these, a handful are job-sharers.

The commitment to flexibility is definitely there. Says Sherry Mosley, a human resources manager with Corning: "We do not have a Mommy Track. Any of our employees on a part-time option are considered for promotion. Women working part-time alternatives have been promoted just like everybody else." At Corning, flexibility can mean being creative with a full-time schedule. Some engineers work full-time, but work from home part of the week. There are also people on compressed schedules, working a forty-hour week in four days' time. Most striking is the fact that part-time people are allowed to have supervisory responsibilities. People on alternative schedules can be and are managers.

New mothers, fathers, and adoptive parents are eligible for the company's twenty-week, job-protected unpaid parental leave option. Corning is the major employer in the small town of Corning, New York. The company helped start a Parent Resource Center within the community, is active in promoting child-care initiatives at the state level, and is represented on a tricounty task force that's looking at sick-child care, after-school care, and day care in general. In 1990, Corning launched a child-care referral program and hired a full-time career-and-family consultant to facilitate the company's work/family programs.

Digital Equipment Corporation
146 Main Street
Maynard, Massachusetts 01754
508-493-5111

Digital Equipment allows part-time, job-sharing, compressed work weeks, flextime, and, to a limited extent, telecommuting. Of 700 people on part-time schedules, 475 are salaried employees at the managerial and professional level. Full benefits are available to part-timers who work thirty hours or more a week. Digital is in the process of revising policies for individual business units, based on proposals that spring from those units. Work-from-home is a case-by-case phenomenon, primarily limited to professionals in the computer area. The company's new parental leave policies were introduced in 1987, adding eight weeks unpaid time off to the standard medical disability leave. That year, about 400 people took advantage of the program; sixty-five of those were men.

With more than 125,000 employees around the world, this hi-tech giant is highly decentralized. So Digital offers different work/family benefits at different locations: some sites offer child care, others resources and referral, others sick care; it depends on the business unit. Right now, corporate employee relations is looking at new, flexible options, including broader applications for telecommuting, seasonal employment, and sabbaticals. The company already has a hardship leave program, allowing employees up to a year off without pay due to a family illness.

Eastman Kodak Company
343 State Street
Rochester, New York 14650
716-724-4000

Kodak has 300 to 500 job-shares—most in routine clerical and administrative functions—and about 1,000 part-time employees. Theirs is thus one of the most widely used alternative-work-schedule programs in American industry. The company's Alternative Work Schedules policy allows for part-time work and job-sharing as well as flexible scheduling to meet an individual's needs and flexibility on a day-to-day basis for emergencies. Part-time employees are eligible for full medical benefits; other benefits are prorated.

Maternity leave, covered under the company's short-term disability program, allows eight to ten weeks of leave with full pay and benefits. The company's family-leave policy provides up to seventeen additional weeks of unpaid, job-protected leave for birth or adoption. The part-time option is available to new mothers returning from family leave. Kodak expanded its work/family programs in 1990 to include adoption assistance, child-care resources and referral, and an employee assistance program. Other work/family policies include a pretax set-aside for child-care expenses, supervisor training, and parenting seminars.

Herman Miller, Inc.
8500 Byron Road
Zeeland, Michigan 49464
616-772-3300

Although this furniture manufacturing company with 5,200 employees has no written policy on job-sharing, Herman Miller encourages alternative approaches and has about sixty job-sharers and nearly 200 part-timers. They include clericals, professionals, and salaried specialists; none are in supervisory roles. Many mothers have converted full-time positions into part-time ones. According to Howard Johnson, director of personnel, they were simply too valuable to lose.

Part-timers are eligible for benefits—including holidays, vacation, pension, profit-sharing, performance bonuses, and prorated medical and dental coverage. New mothers who've been with Herman Miller two or more years receive full compensation during a six- to eight-week disability leave; they're allowed up to three months additional unpaid time off at a supervisor's discretion. Men are also eligible for unpaid leave. It's not uncommon for new mothers to return part-time. Newborns receive a gift from the company—a rocking chair or $100 savings bond. We say, take the bond.

Hewlett-Packard Company
3000 Hanover Street
Palo Alto, California 94304
415-857-1501

With 93,000 people worldwide and 300 U.S. locations, Hewlett-Packard is no small company. Yet, this manufacturer of measurement and computation products has managed to introduce a fair amount of flexibility into the workplace. Flextime is in place company-wide. At headquarters, which operates on an eight-hour day, employees may start work any time between 6 A.M. and 8:30 A.M. Manufacturing sites have more restrictive hours, which vary by location. The company's flexible time-off policy allows employees to combine their annual vacation leave and sick leave into a bank of hours, which they can use for any purpose. While there is no official job-sharing program, we found ten job-sharing pairs at Hewlett-Packard. Both telecommuting and job-sharing options are decided on a case-by-case basis; much is left in the hands of individual supervisors.

Most surprising is the extent to which salaried people are working reduced hours. There are 585 regular part-timers at HP in the United States—forty of them are in supervisory roles and more than half are in salaried positions. Regular part-timers who work twenty or more hours a week receive prorated benefits, including health insurance coverage, and participate in the company's merit-pay, stock-purchase, 401-K, retirement, and profit-sharing programs. In order to open the way for more part-time arrangements, Hewlett-Packard has changed its headcount rules—a part-timer no longer counts as one person in the budgeting process. The company also changed the benefits policies to make part-time more cost effective; in the old days, part-timers were eligible for full benefits—that's no longer the case.

Hewlett-Packard allows up to two months unpaid parental leave in addition to standard medical disability. The company also offers a pretax salary set-aside for dependent care.

Hoffmann-La Roche, Inc.
340 Kingsland Street
Nutley, New Jersey 07110
201-235-5000

Hoffmann-La Roche, a leading research-intensive health-care company based in Nutley, New Jersey, has strong work/family programs that include flextime, job-sharing, part-time work options, child-care services, and family-issues counseling and referral. According to company officials, "many" Roche employees job-share and thousands of employees are on part-time schedules, including administrative, technical, and professional people. Employees who work sixteen or more hours a week are eligible to participate in the company benefits plan. While some benefits are prorated, part-timers are eligible for 100 percent health coverage.

There are no senior-level executives who make use of alternative work options. A written, company-wide policy regarding job-sharing allows hourly, salaried, exempt, and nonexempt employees, including people at the professional level, to participate in job-shares, provided the arrangement meets with a supervisor's approval. However, management-level employees are not eligible for job-sharing arrangements.

A company-wide flextime policy, with core hours of 9 A.M. to 3 P.M., is implemented at the discretion of individual managers and may vary by location.

In addition to standard disability leave, Roche has an unpaid parental leave of three months—adoptive parents and fathers are eligible—as well as a one-year personal leave policy.

In 1989, Hoffmann-La Roche was named one of ten best U.S. employers for women by *Working Mother* magazine. A leader in providing child-care services, Roche was the first company in New Jersey and one of the first in the nation to provide corporate-sponsored, tuition-subsidized, on-site child care. At corporate headquarters in Nutley, Roche offers numerous child-care options, including full-time child care for preschoolers up through kindergarten; a state-licensed kindergarten program; part-time care for school-age children; a full-time summer program; emergency care and a drop-in program for preschoolers. Other Roche services include an employee information network to help families locate child care in their home communities. The Concerned Women of Roche, with 700 active members, is reputed to be the oldest women's support group in U.S. industry.

Honeywell, Inc.
Honeywell Plaza
Minneapolis, Minnesota 55408
612-870-5200

Honeywell, the international electronics company based in Minneapolis, has some unusually progressive personal time off policies. For example, there is technically no limit of the amount of paid time off an employee can take to care for a sick child; it's completely up to the supervisor. Another example: headquarters employees may take up to sixty days off with pay for death or serious illness in the immediate family, provided the human resources department approves. The company's flexible unpaid leave-of-absence policy was revised in 1989. It allows Minneapolis-based employees to begin a six-month adoption, maternity, or paternity leave at any time within the first six months following a birth. In other words, if a new mother comes back to work after her disability leave and wishes she hadn't, she can go back home on personal leave. During that time, employment is guaranteed, job grade is maintained, and benefits stay in place.

In 1988, Honeywell established a task force to look at work/family issues. That year, the company conducted an extensive survey of the child-care needs of 7,000 Minneapolis-based employees. Sick care emerged as a major concern, and in September 1988 the company unveiled a sick-care policy. Honeywell not only allows employees paid time off to care for sick kids, but also offers access to an in-home sitter service. The company pays 80 percent of the cost of that service—$10.80 an hour to the employee's $2.70.

What about flexible jobs? About half the company's headquarters employees are on flextime schedules. While the 1988 survey also pointed to an interest in flexibility, at this writing, flexible jobs are not a priority at Honeywell. Right now, most of these policies apply only to Minneapolis-based people. But Honeywell formed a corporation-wide work-and-family-life committee in the spring of 1990 to consider programs throughout the corporation. Other work/family supports include child-care resources and referral in Minneapolis and discounts for area day care.

International Business Machines Corporation
IBM United States
2000 Purchase Street
Purchase, New York 10577-2597
914-697-6626

IBM's parental leave policy, announced in 1988, sets the standard against which most corporations are measured. Employees may take to up to three years unpaid leave, during which the company pays full benefits coverage. Those away one year will be given their old or a comparable job. Every effort is made to do the same for those absent more than a year. New mothers have the option of arranging a part-time return to work; those who take advantage of the extended leave program are required to make themselves available for part-time work in years two and three. The company also has a pilot work-from-home program in place for people on leave who want to work from home. Indeed, IBM's main thrust appears to be that of making life easier for new mothers. Aside from privately negotiated arrangements, these part-time and work-from-home options are designed primarily for people who have been out on leave.

IBM allows flextime, staggered hours, and customized work schedules. As of May 1990, there was no formal job-sharing program. IBM's flextime, or "Individualized Work Schedule" program, allows for an hour of flexibility on arrival and departure, and includes a midday window of flexibility at two pilot locations.

The company contracts with Massachusetts-based Work/Family Directions to provide child-care and eldercare referral services nationwide and has an extraordinarily generous fund of $25 million in place to support community-based child-care and eldercare initiatives throughout the country.

Johnson & Johnson
One Johnson & Johnson Plaza
New Brunswick, New Jersey 08933
908-524-0400

In 1989, after studying work/family programs at other companies and surveying Johnson & Johnson employees, this consumer products company unveiled a comprehensive program of its own. Johnson & Johnson's new work/family program includes two on-site day-care centers at New Jersey locations, a nationwide resources and referral network for child care and eldercare, and flexible work policies allowing job-sharing and part-time. As of 1990, there are a handful of job-sharers at the company's New Jersey headquarters and at least some part-time professional and management-level jobs—numbers were not available to us. As of April 1991, part-timers became eligible for a wide range of benefits, including health coverage.

Men are eligible for Johnson & Johnson's family-care leave, which can be used to care for any family member; unpaid leave time is granted for up to a year with an employment guarantee; the same job is guaranteed for three months. The company encourages managers to come up with creative arrangements for new mothers returning from leave, including work-from-home situations on a part- and full-time basis. Supervisor training is part of the package. Other work/family programs unveiled in 1989 include adoption assistance and a pretax salary set-aside for child care. In the summer of 1989, the company introduced flextime at its headquarters for the first time.

However comprehensive, all of these programs are very new for Johnson & Johnson. The policies, outlined in a work/family kit, are definitely in place; what remains is for these work/family supports to become part of the corporate culture. Says Chris Kjeldsen, vice-president of headquarters human resources: "In a few years these programs are going to be very much a part of our environment." That is something only time will tell.

Levi Strauss & Co.
Levi's Plaza
PO Box 7215
San Francisco, California 94120-6916
415-544-6000

When the Conference Board conducted its survey of 500-plus member corporations, they found only four firms that offered flexibility in every category studied, from job-sharing to work from home. Levi Strauss was one of them. The San Francisco–based blue-jean maker allows job-sharing, part-time, work-from-home, flexible scheduling, flextime, and compressed work weeks at its headquarters, provided the arrangement has supervisor approval.

At Levi Strauss, we found evidence that flexibility doesn't have to impede one's career growth. The senior vice-president of personnel at Levi Strauss is the highest-ranking woman at the company. She took a year off when she had her first child and six months off when she had her second. At one point in her career, she worked three days a week at Levi Strauss. Then she worked four days a week. Now that she's a senior vice-president, Donna Goya works full-time.

Part-timers on the home-office payroll who work twenty hours or more a week are eligible for the regular benefits. Levi Strauss allows up to five months of child-care leave—combining standard paid disability and additional unpaid leave time. An employee's job is guaranteed for sixty days; following that, every effort is made to find a comparable job. Paid time off for family sick care can be taken in daily or hourly increments. The company is hooked into a vast statewide resources and referral service in California, offers pretax child-care subsidies, and provides a resource library for parents at its San Francisco headquarters.

At present, the work/family programs and flexible guidelines outlined here apply only to the 2,700 employees on the home-office payroll. But in 1990, Levi Strauss launched a company-wide survey to develop new work/family policies for its entire domestic work force of 27,000. Says Meg Franklin, manager of benefits services: "We don't know what the survey's going to show. People might say, 'We need child care.' Different areas have different needs, so we might create different programs for different places." As evidence of the company's commitment to change, Bob Haas, chairman of the board and chief executive officer, sits on the company's seventeen-member work/family task force.

Merck and Co., Inc.
PO Box 2000
Rahway, New Jersey 07065
908-574-4000

Merck and Co., the New Jersey–based pharmaceutical company with 32,000 employees in eighteen countries, consistently wins recognition for its progressive personnel policies. The company conducted its first survey of employees' work/family needs in 1984, making it one of the first corporations to do so. Flextime has been in place at Merck since 1981—the core hours are 10 A.M. to 3:30 P.M., and, according to data gathered by the Families and Work Institute, 50 percent of the company's headquarters employees take advantage of the option. Merck's flexible work policies are designed primarily to accommodate new mothers returning from leave. The child care leave itself can be stretched to eighteen months' unpaid leave with an employment guarantee, six months with a job guarantee. Men are eligible. Supervisors are encouraged to be creative in accommodating returning mothers with part-time and work-from-home arrangements. Beyond that, it's difficult to tell how supportive the company is in workplace flexibility. Job-sharing, while allowed, is not widespread. Part-time work has reached the middle-management level—benefits are prorated.

Minnesota Mining & Manufacturing Co. (3M)
3M Center
St. Paul, Minnesota 55144
612-733-1110

3M clearly has work/family on its agenda. At headquarters in St. Paul, Minnesota, the company provides subsidized care for mildly ill children through 3M-approved providers, discounted rates at an area summer camp, child-care information services, and parent-education seminars. A full-time employee is assigned the task of consulting with parents on child care and other family issues. Child-care referral services are also available at some 3M locations throughout the United States. As for flexibility, 3M allows flextime (core hours are 9 A.M. to 3 P.M.), part-time, job-sharing, and, in a few rare cases, telecommuting. Benefits are prorated. Most part-time arrangements or job-shares are viewed as temporary solutions, however, designed primarily for mothers coming back from maternity leave. New mothers can take up to two months unpaid leave—it's called "special leave"—in addition to standard medical disability, with an employment guarantee; fathers and adoptive parents are also eligible. Extensions and the option of a part-time return are up to individual supervisors. In addition, five paid days are granted each year for family emergencies.

Morrison & Foerster
345 California Street
San Francisco, California 94104-2675
415-677-7000

The nation's twelfth largest law firm, Morrison & Foerster has a history of leadership in the work/family arena. Secretaries and other administrative staffers can work staggered hours or part-time or job-share. Part-timers are eligible for health, disability, and family sick-leave benefits at thirty hours. Employees may use their ten sick days accrued annually to care for a sick family member. Attorneys may adopt a flexible work schedule—that is, reduced hours—for up to twelve months, *provided* they use that time to be with their children. As of April 1990, only two of the firm's 190 partners and eleven of the 345 associates are on part-time schedules. In all, seventy-three of the firm's 1,524 employees work part-time. Of those, seven are job-sharers.

Until recently, Morrison & Foerster had separate disability leave policies for attorneys and staffers. Staffers were not covered under the firm's disability leave program; they had to rely instead on state programs or accrued vacation and sick days for paid time off following childbirth. But that changed on January 1, 1990, when Morrison & Foerster became one of the first law firms to extend short-term disability benefits of up to ninety days to all employees with one year or more of service. Employees with more than five years of service are eligible for leave at full salary.

In addition, lawyers are eligible for a three-month *unpaid* leave of absence in connection with childbirth; this unpaid leave time must be taken within ninety days of the date of birth or adoption. Under the firm's leave-of-absence policy, other full-time employees are eligible for ninety days *unpaid* leave for personal reasons; during that time, employees who elect to continue their health insurance coverage must pay for it, and, while there are no guarantees, every effort is made to ensure reemployment.

Morrison & Foerster also provides pretax salary set-asides for child care, offers work/family seminars, and is actively involved in the San Francisco Bay Area Child Care Coalition, which helps area employers develop work/family policies. The firm plans to add an on-site weekend drop-in child-care center at its San Francisco offices.

Northeast Utilities
PO Box 270
Hartford, Connecticut 06141-0270
203-665-5000

Back in 1982, Northeast Utilities, the power company that provides electric service in Connecticut and western Massachusetts, began developing a job-sharing program. The company developed job-sharing guidelines, contracts, benefits policies, and self-evaluation sheets for prospective job-sharers. From 1984 to 1985, the utility conducted a pilot project involving eight job-sharing teams. "We held everybody's hands through the first year," says Mike Brown, director of employee relations. The result, according to Brown, was a resounding success. The company's official job-sharing policy went into effect December 1, 1986. Today, there are 108 job-sharers and about forty part-timers—including engineers, accountants, secretaries, meter readers, and analysts of various types. The only restriction: people who job-share or work part-time are not allowed to have supervisory responsibilities. That too may change in time, Brown speculates.

Northeast's variable work schedule program allows for flexible scheduling; core hours are 9:30 A.M. to 2 P.M. Employees can arrive as early at 6 A.M. Compressed work weeks are also an option at Northeast. Telecommuting, however, remains rare and is used only in cases where an employee is sick or disabled. In the 1980s, aside from piloting its job-sharing program, the company changed its benefits policies to accommodate part-timers, who are now eligible for full health coverage at twenty or more hours a week. Part-timers have the option of paying for dependent coverage. Other benefits are prorated.

The parental leave policy allows up to six months unpaid time off (benefits are continued during the first month of absence). Other work/family supports include child-care and eldercare resources and referral. As of 1990, Northeast was looking at its sick-care policies to allow employees more flexibility to care for sick kids.

Pioneer Hi-Bred International, Inc.
400 Locust Street
700 Capital Square
Des Moines, Iowa 50309
515-245-3500

You might not expect a midwestern company in the agricultural business to rank among the most flexible U.S. firms, but Des Moines–based Pioneer Hi-Bred, the world's largest seed company, is just that. With 8,000 full-time-equivalent employees, Pioneer Hi-Bred has about 2,500 part-time people, including fifty to seventy-five job-sharers. Several years ago, chief executive officer and president Tom Urban read an article about alternative schedules in the *Wall Street Journal* and asked his human resources people to look into what other companies were doing. As a result, the company published guidelines for supervisors, encouraging them to explore alternative work arrangements; benefits were extended to people who work 1,000 or more hours a year. In April 1990, at Tom Urban's suggestion, alternative schedules were included in the employee handbook for the first time, to encourage even more flexibility.

Job-sharing, part-time, flextime, compressed work weeks, extended work weeks (a six-day week with shorter days), and telecommuting are all options. Many of the company's forty production facilities and forty research stations are on flextime scheduling. Several plants employ compressed work weeks. About thirty people, primarily in the computer area, are telecommuting. According to Lisa Mullan, manager for the computer division, the programs have not necessarily been targeted to women. But, as women are beginning to move up through the ranks of Pioneer Hi-Bred, traditionally a male-dominated firm in a male-dominated industry, they're beginning to take advantage of some of this flexibility. While job-sharing is encouraged, it is still restricted primarily to clerical, administrative, and technical jobs. And, although there are no executive-level part-timers or job-sharers, there are professionals who are job-sharing or working part-time or compressed work weeks.

Steelcase, Inc.
PO Box 1967
Grand Rapids, Michigan 49501
616-247-2710

At Steelcase, Inc., a Michigan-based furniture manufacturer, job-sharing, flextime, and part-time options have become a widely accepted part of the corporate culture. The company has offered job-sharing to salaried employees since 1982, and today it is one of the few American companies that actually post job-share positions to help employees find partners. Job-sharing teams and part-timers have earned promotions into higher-level flexible jobs. While plenty of professionals and management-level people work on reduced schedules, part-timers and job-sharers are not allowed to have supervisory or budgetary responsibilities. As of July 1990, there are ninety-four job-sharers and forty-five part-timers—many of them in salaried positions.

At Steelcase, part-time and job-sharing extend beyond the office walls to the company's U.S. manufacturing sites. Hourly employees became eligible for job-sharing and part-time schedules in 1988. "So you've got quality control inspectors, hi-lo drivers, sweepers, and assemblers working part-time and sharing jobs," says Joe Pearce, employee relations manager, "along with product engineers and sales managers." From the company's perspective, the benefits of flexibility include a phenomenally low turnover rate of 3 percent.

Factory employees are not eligible for flextime, and flextime schedules for office workers vary from one department to another; core hours are 9 to 11:15 and 1:15 to 3. The company is not above experimenting with flexibility. Consider this example: the graveyard shift—4 P.M. to 4 A.M.—in the customer service and order entry departments operates on a system called "Total Flex." Basically, it's a schedule of staggered arrival times agreed on in advance by the employees themselves. There are no core hours. Two people come in at 5 P.M., two more at 6 P.M., and so forth into the night.

Job-sharers receive a prorated salary and split the benefits package that goes with the job; but they can buy the additional half for a full health benefits package if needed. As for parental leave, new mothers, fathers, and adoptive parents can take up to ninety days unpaid leave. Employees may use their sick days to care for sick children. Other work/family benefits include child-care resources and referral in the Grand Rapids area, adoption assistance, and a pretax salary set-aside for dependent care. Steelcase food service sells take-home dinners, party platters, and decorated cakes, a definite plus for working parents.

Time Inc. Magazines
Time Warner
1271 Avenue of the Americas
New York, New York 10020
212-522-1212

People at Time Inc. Magazines sometimes work odd hours. A three-day week consisting of fourteen- or sixteen-hour days is not unheard of. That's the nature of the deadline-oriented business of putting out weekly magazines. But Time's interest in flexibility goes beyond scheduling to meet the needs of the business: managers are encouraged to accommodate people's needs. Part-time, job-sharing, and work-from-home are all options. There are a handful of job-sharers at the company's New York and L.A. offices. More common are full-time arrangements with a high degree of flexibility.

Company policy allows for a one-year unpaid parental leave with a continuation of medical coverage; every effort is made to hold the same or a comparable job. A gradual or part-time return from leave is allowed, and creative solutions, including work-from-home combined with part-time office work, are encouraged.

Time's magazine division has a history of leadership in work/family. Other family-supportive policies in the magazine division include childcare and eldercare referral, work/family workshops and support groups, a pretax salary set-aside program for dependent-care, and adoption assistance. Time is participating in an innovative pilot program that offers emergency care for sick kids to parents in New York and New Jersey and has published a booklet outlining work/family policies for supervisors and employees. During the pilot phase, in-home sitters for sick kids have been available to Time's magazine group employees at no charge. Karol Rose, a full-time work/family consultant, has been on board since 1986. Following the merger of Time and Warner Communications, Rose was promoted from manager of work-and-family programs at Time Inc. Magazines to the same post within Time Warner, so she'll be working with divisions and operating units throughout Time Warner to come up with new, localized work/family supports.

The Travelers Corp.
One Tower Square
Hartford, Connecticut 06183-1060
203-277-0111

The Travelers Corporation, one of the world's largest multiline insurance, financial services, managed health-care, and investment companies, has been a leader in providing supports for eldercare and offering alternative schedules to retirees and employees. Since 1981, the Travelers Retiree Job Bank has offered part-time and temporary employment. In 1990, the Job Bank became part of Travelers new in-house temporary agency, employing both retirees and other temporary workers. The company has had a formal flextime program since 1984 (core hours are 9 to 9:30). Part-timers who work seventeen and a half hours or more a week are eligible for company benefits. Other alternative work programs including job-sharing, which is considered on a case-by-case basis, and telecommuting, which may be done on a full- or part-time basis. Telecommuters are required to come into the office one day a week.

In January 1990, Travelers expanded its work/family programs to include subsidies for child-care or eldercare expenses, up to one year of unpaid family leave, nationwide eldercare and child-care referral, and three paid days off for family care.

US Sprint (A Unit of United Telecommunications, Inc.)
8140 Ward Parkway
Kansas City, Missouri 64114
816-276-6000

The company proposed, launched, and implemented a comprehensive work/family initiative in only five months' time. US Sprint's new Workplace Flexibility program is part of the broader Family Care program that took effect in August 1989. The policy allows for flexible hours to meet individual needs, staggered hours and flextime (core hours of 10 A.M. to 2 P.M. are recommended as a guideline), compressed work weeks, job-sharing, and regular part-time with prorated benefits at twenty hours a week. After the program's first full year, 60 percent of Sprint's departments had adopted at least one of the flexible options. US Sprint's flexday policy enables hourly employees to take paid time off in two-hour increments by setting aside one floating holiday per year as a flexday.

The company's Family Care leave policy allows for a one-year unpaid leave for family needs with an employment guarantee. Other elements of the new program include child-care and eldercare resources and referral, an employee assistance program, and a liberal working-partner relocation assistance program.

U S West, Inc.
7800 East Orchard Road
Englewood, Colorado 80111
303-793-6500

When U S West surveyed its employees in 1987, the company found that the number one work/family support people wanted was flexibility. Today, U S West, the Baby Bell that operates in fourteen western states, may well be the most flexible major corporation in the United States. The company encourages flexibility through its Flexible Work Arrangements program, which promotes job-sharing, part-time work, compressed work weeks, flextime, and flexible scheduling, and makes telecommuting a priority. The company's flextime program enables employees throughout U S West's forty-plus market and service units and subsidiaries to become actively involved in setting their own core hours, through work groups and self-managed teams. There are many telecommuters throughout the company, and at least one subsidiary is more than 22 percent telecommuters. While job-sharing is encouraged, U S West doesn't track such arrangements, so numbers aren't available. There are about 1,200 part-timers throughout the company; all are eligible for full benefits and some are in managerial and professional-level jobs.

In 1989, U S West introduced one of the most liberal leave programs in U.S. industry. Called "enhanced leave," it allows for twelve months' unpaid leave—for newborn care, family care, adoption, education—with continued benefits coverage paid for 100 percent by the company. That includes medical and dental coverage, as well as death benefits and even tuition assistance. As of March 1990, that leave can be extended for an additional twelve months, provided the request is approved by the benefits committee. Returning mothers have the option of working part-time or working from home, provided it's feasible from a business perspective. U S West urges mothers working from home to get child-care assistance. Says Dee Vellinga, director of dependent care for U S West: "We more than strongly recommend that telecommuters not have their children with them full-time."

Other work-family supports include a pretax set-aside for child care, a benefit expanded to include all U.S. employees in January 1991, and nationwide resources and referral for child care for most employees. The U S West Foundation has established a $25-million fund for community education, $10 million of it committed to early-childhood initiatives in the fourteen states where the company operates.

Warner-Lambert Company
201 Tabor Road
Morris Plains, New Jersey 07950
201-540-2000

This international health-care and consumer products company allows individually negotiated arrangements and encourages some forms of flexibility. Flextime has been in place at all U.S. locations since the late 1970s, and recently the company expanded its flextime program to allow employees more leeway in changing their hours on a daily basis. There are about sixty people working part-time at all levels of the organization at the company's New Jersey headquarters. They include two attorneys sharing a job, as well as clericals, professionals, and middle-level managers. According to Raymond Fino, corporate vice-president of human resources, job-sharing has worked well and the company is encouraging managers to consider more job-sharing where appropriate. Warner-Lambert will consider work-from-home arrangements, particularly in cases where a new mother is returning from maternity leave. As of August 1990, part-timers at Warner-Lambert were not eligible for health insurance coverage.

Other work/family programs at Warner-Lambert include a nationwide resources and referral service for child care and eldercare. Of the twelve sick days available each year, five may be used to care for a sick dependent. The company's unpaid parental leave policy allows for a ninety-day leave with continued benefits and a job guarantee; a part-time return is a possibility. Warner-Lambert's relocation program includes career counseling for trailing spouses and school match services for children of relocating employees. According to company officials, Warner-Lambert also makes a substantial investment in training managers to be sensitive to family issues.

THE FLEXIBLE OPTIONS: A GLOSSARY

COMPRESSED WORK WEEK   An employee on a compressed work week does a full-time or forty-hour-a-week job in less than five days. A typical compressed work week consists of four ten-hour days. A common variation is a two-week schedule made up of five nine-hour days, followed by a week of four nine-hour days.

EXTENDED WORK WEEK   An extended work week involves stretching a thirty-five- or forty-hour week over more than five days. The most common arrangement is a six-day week made up of shorter workdays.

FLEXIBLE SCHEDULE   We use this term for a schedule that is tailored to the needs of an individual employee. For example, a person might be allowed to arrive late and work late every Wednesday for some personal reason; he or she might work shorter hours several days a week or even come and go as he or she pleases. Some progressive companies are encouraging managers and supervisors to be open to a variety of scheduling options to accommodate employee needs.

FLEXTIME (ALSO *FLEX-TIME, FLEXITIME*)   Flextime allows employees to vary their starting and quitting times while still working a standard seven-and-a-half- or eight-hour day. Some companies provide a two- or three-hour leeway on starting and quitting times (called a flexband); others provide as little as thirty minutes of flexibility. Midday flexbands, where employees can lengthen or shorten their lunch break, are also an option. *Core hours* are the times when employees are required to be at work. A typical flextime policy might allow an eight-hour day to begin as early as 7 A.M. and as late as 9 A.M., with core hours of 9 A.M. to 3 P.M.

JOB-SHARING   A form of part-time work, job-sharing allows two people to share the duties of one full-time position. Generally, salaries and benefits are prorated based on the number of hours each person works.

LEAVE   Leave time—paid or unpaid—is authorized time away from work. Paid leave includes vacations, sabbaticals, and disability leaves (paid maternity leave generally falls under a company's disability leave policy). Unpaid leave policies—including leaves of absence, personal leaves, parental leaves, family leaves, and infant-care leaves—vary dramatically from company to company as to benefits coverage, job guarantees, and retention of seniority, as well as the length and reasons allowed for leave.

PART-TIME WORK   Technically, a part-time employee is anyone who works thirty or fewer hours a week in any combination of days or hours. Most part-time employees have job security and are eligible for some benefits.

SHORTENED HOURS, SHORTENED WORK WEEKS   Because of the limited definition of part-time work and the stigma attached to the part-time label, we've used these terms throughout the book. *Shortened hours* refers to a five-day-a-week schedule with a shorter workday—that might mean, for example, working five seven-hour days. *Shortened work week* might involve working two, three, or even four and a half days a week. When you begin talking about managerial and professional jobs, traditional ideas about part-time *hours* becomes less useful. Many of the new "part-timers" are salaried, not hourly, employees and they may travel or put in extra time on the days they work.

STAGGERED HOURS   Refers to a standard seven-and-a-half or eight-hour workday with a fixed schedule that falls outside the norm—say, a regular 7 A.M. to 4 P.M. workday that is in effect every day.

TELECOMMUTING (ALSO *FLEXIPLACE, WORK-FROM-HOME*)   All of these terms refer to work arrangements where the employee spends all or part of his or her working hours at home. The term *telecommuting* literally refers to employees who communicate back to the office via computer. However, it can also refer to arrangements where the telephone is the only equipment needed and is sometimes used as the generic term for working from home.

GUIDE TO RESOURCES

NATIONAL ORGANIZATIONS

Accountemps/Robert Half International
2884 Sandhill Road, Suite 200
Menlo Park, CA 94025
415-854-9700
    Temporary placement firm for accountants, with offices nationwide.

Association of Part-Time Professionals
7700 Leesburg Pike, Suite 216
Falls Church, VA 22043
703-734-7975
    A national nonprofit membership organization that provides information
and resources on flexible work arrangements. Main focus is the Washington, D.C., area; however, it is expanding and currently has local chapters
in Boston and Hampton, New Hampshire.

Bureau of National Affairs
1231 25th Street, N.W.
Washington, DC 20037
800-372-1033 or 202-452-4200
> A private publisher of specialized information on employee relations, environment and safety, law, taxation, and business and economics. Publishes special report series on work and family and hosts annual conference.

Catalyst
250 Park Avenue South, 5th Floor
New York, NY 10003-1459
212-777-8900
> A nationally based nonprofit organization that primarily works with businesses to effect change for women through research, advisory services, and communication. They have an extensive publications list that includes in-depth information about flexible work as well as career development resources.

Clearinghouse on Work and Family
Women's Bureau, U.S. Department of Labor
200 Constitution Avenue, N.W.
Washington, DC 20210
202-523-4486
> Provides research on work and family issues.

Conference Board Inc.
Work and Family Information Center
845 Third Avenue
New York, NY 10022
212-759-0900 or 212-339-0377
> Provides information to senior executives on work/family-related issues.

Families and Work Institute
330 Seventh Avenue
New York, NY 10001
212-465-2044
Nonprofit organization focusing on policy research and corporate strategic planning. Serves as a national clearinghouse for information on work/family issues and develops training programs and educational materials for clients in government and business. Publisher of *Corporate Reference Guide,* outlining work/family policies and programs at some 200 U.S. corporations.

Family Resource Coalition
230 North Michigan Avenue, Suite 1625
Chicago, IL 60601
312-726-4750
A national nonprofit federation of more than 2,000 individuals and organizations promoting the development of prevention-oriented, community-based programs to strengthen families. They produce numerous publications, including work/family program resource kits for employers.

Family Service America
11700 West Lake Park Drive, Park Place
Milwaukee, WI 53224
414-359-1040
Provides referrals nationwide to individuals seeking work/family counseling.

Gil Gordon Associates
10 Donner Court
Monmouth Junction, NJ 08852
201-329-2266
Telecommuting consulting services. Publishes *Telecommuting Review: The Gordon Report,* a newsletter on trends and legislation.

National Association For Women in Careers
PO Box 4254
Northbrook, IL 60065
708-657-5422
> Provides workshops, newsletter, flexible job counseling, and referrals for women.

National Council for Research on Women
47–49 East 65th Street
New York, NY 10021
212-570-5001
> Provides research on women's issues.

National Council of Jewish Women
Center for the Child
53 W. 23rd Street
New York, NY 10010
212-645-4048
> Research on the subject of balancing work and family.

New Ways to Work
149 Ninth Street
San Francisco, CA 94103
415-552-1000
> A work resource center that conducts research, serves as a clearinghouse for information on alternative work arrangements, and promotes flexible work options.

9 to 5
National Association of Working Women
614 Superior Avenue, N.W.
Cleveland, OH 44113
216-566-9308
> Membership organization for office workers. Operates Job Survival Hotline (1-800-245-9865). Trained job counselors respond to questions about flexible jobs, maternity leave, and balancing work and family between 10:00 A.M. and 4:30 P.M.

Parent Action
PO Box 1719
Washington, DC 20013
202-835-2016
  Membership organization providing support to parents and advocacy of issues of priority to them.

Project on Home-Based Work
Graduate School & University Center
City University of New York
33 West 42nd Street
New York, NY 10036
212-642-2530
  Research on home-based work.

Resources for Child Care Management
261 Springfield Avenue, Suite 201
Berkeley Heights, NJ 07922
201 665 9070
  Child-care consultant to corporations. Hosts an annual conference on employer supports for child care and publishes *BusinessLink*, a quarterly newsletter on new corporate initiatives that address the needs of working parents.

Roosevelt Center for American Policy Studies
4301 13th St., N.W.
Washington, DC 20011
202-576-6130
  A nonprofit, nonpartisan public policy institute that conducts various research. Of particular interest is their Balancing Work and Family Project.

U.S. Government Office of Personnel Management
Pay and Leave Administrator
1900 E Street, N.W.
Washington, DC 20415-0001
202-606-2858
  Information and research on flexible jobs within the federal government.

Wellesley College Center for Research on Women
Wellesley College
Wellesley, MA 02181
617-235-0320 or 617-235-6360
> The Center for Research on Women conducts research on various topics concerning women. They have an extensive publications list.

Work and Family Life Seminar Program
Bank Street College of Education
610 West 112th Street
New York, NY 10025
212-222-6700
> Provides bag-lunch seminars on a wide variety of work/family issues.

Work and Family Resources
15680 37th Street South
Afton, MN 55001
612-436-7968
> Provides consultation, surveys, and strategy development to companies on work/family issues. Develops curricula with companies for lunchtime seminars.

Work/Family Directions, Inc.
9 Galen Street, Suite 230
Watertown, MA 02172
617-235-6222 or 617-923-1535
> Corporate consultant whose services include research, strategic planning, and nationwide child-care and eldercare referral. Produces seminars and educational materials.

NORTH CENTRAL

A Better Way, Inc., Strategies
31313 Northwestern Highway, #113
Farmington Hills, MI 48018
313-855-6000
> Produces large annual conference on women's career issues. Consults on work/family issues.

Klivans, Becker & Smith
3091 Mayfield Road, Suite 310
Cleveland, OH 44113
216-932-7256
Placement firm for management-level temporaries.

Lucia Landon
8301 Stateline Road
Kansas City, MO 64114
816-363-1518
Consultant on work/family issues.

Minnesota Work and Family Institute
Hennepin Technical Institute
1820 North Xenium Lane
Plymouth, MN 55441
612-553-5655
Provides seminars on family and parenting issues statewide.

Of Counsel Inc.
4149 Pennsylvania, Suite 306
Kansas City, MO 64111
816-753-4644
A placement firm that provides paralegals and lawyers to law firms on a part-time and temporary basis.

Personnel Projects
2615 Xylon Avenue South
St. Louis Park, MN 55426
612-545-3178
Provides workshops on work/family issues to the Twin Cities metropolitan area.

Women Employed Institute
22 West Monroe, Suite 1400
Chicago, IL 60603
312-782-3902
A membership organization providing career development counseling and seminars. It also offers support groups and a job bank.

Work and Family Spectrum
1006 West Lake Street
Minneapolis, MN 55408
612-370-9435 or 612-627-2927
    Provides lunchtime seminars on work/family issues.

Working Parent Resource Center
Town Square, North Central Life Tower
445 Minnesota Ave., #520
St. Paul, MN 55101
612-293-5330
    Provides services to downtown working parents, including lunchtime seminars, a resource library, and consultation for parent educators.

NORTHEAST

Administrative Management Society
4622 Street Road
Trevose, PA 19047
215-953-1040
    Conducts annual survey of flexible jobs.

Alternatrack
641 Lexington Avenue
New York, NY 10022
212-688-2793
    Placement firm for professionals in financial services. Specializes in providing flexible jobs.

Association of Part-Time Professionals
PO Box 65
Newton, MA 02164
617-965-7119 or 508-686-5707
    Northeast chapter of the Association of Part-Time Professionals, a national nonprofit membership organization that provides information and resources on flexible work arrangements.

Career Development Services
Temple Building, Suite 1200
14 Franklin Street
Rochester, NY 14604-1504
716-325-2274
Provides job counseling to individuals on balancing work and family.

Career Transition Resources
26 Court Street, Suite 610
Brooklyn Heights, NY 11242
718-624-3192
Career counselors specializing in assisting parents in balancing work and family.

Careers Unlimited
39 Windsor Road
Great Neck, NY 11021
516-773-4204
Provides comprehensive career assessment and counseling.

Center for Parenting Studies
Wheelock College
200 The Riverway
Boston, MA 02215
617-734-5200
Provides companies with intensive on-site management seminars.

Center for Research and Education in the Workplace
University of Pennsylvania School of Social Work
3701 Locust Walk
Philadelphia, PA 19104
215-898-7910
Provides research on balancing work and family.

Executive Corner
99 Jericho Turnpike
Jericho, NY 11753
516-333-2121
Placement firm for management-level temporaries.

The Experts
1 Washington Street
Wellesley, MA 02181
617-237-1777
    Placement agency for computer consultants.

Freelancers Over 50
501 Cambridge Street
Cambridge, MA 02141
617-354-4102
    A nonprofit placement firm for professionals over fifty, part-time, or freelance job seekers.

Hilda Lee Dail & Associates, International
320 East 57th Street, Apt. 3F
New York, NY 10022
212-752-1195
    Career counselors utilizing a program called "How to Create Your Own Career."

Institute for Women and Work
N.Y. State School of Industrial and Labor Relations
Cornell University
15 East 26th Street
New York, NY 10010
212-340-2800
    Research on women in the workplace.

Interim Management Corp.
470 Park Avenue South
New York, NY 10016
212-213-3600
    Placement firm for management-level temporaries.

Management Assistance Group
10 N. Main Street
West Hartford, CT 06107
203-523-0000
   Placement firm for management-level temporaries.

Operation Able of Greater Boston
World Trade Center, Suite 306
Boston, MA 02210-2078
617-439-5580
   A private, nonprofit firm that counsels over-forty-five job seekers. Facilitates full or part-time positions.

Options, Inc.
215 South Broad Street
Philadelphia, PA 19107
215-735-2202
   A consulting firm providing services to individuals and employers interested in flexible work arrangements.

The Partnership Group
840 West Main Street
Lansdale, PA 19446
215-362-5070
   Referral agency specializing in alternative work styles.

Pickwick Group
110 Cedar Street
Wellesley Hills, MA 02180
617-235-6222
   A placement agency for temporary and part-time professional and managerial staff.

Princeton Entrepreneurial Resources
PO Box 2051
Princeton, NJ 08543
609-243-0010
   Placement firm for management-level temporaries.

Resources for Parents at Work
7212 Lincoln Drive
Philadelphia, PA 19119
> Provides educational seminars on child development, parent education, stress reduction, and balancing work and family life. Offers counseling for executives on work/family issues.

Staff Alternative
65 Glenbrook Road, #11B
Stamford, CT 06902
203-323-3777
> Placement firm for executives interested in part-time or short-term work assignments.

Susanne Parente Associates, Inc.
516 North Avenue East
Westfield, NJ 07090
201-233-8020
> Career development counselors specializing in spouse relocation.

Vera Sullivan Associates
1641 Third Avenue, Suite 8FE
New York, NY 10218-3623
212-427-5717 or 212-348-3431
> Provides career counseling and assistance in balancing work and family.

Wheelock College Center for Parenting Studies
200 The Riverway
Boston, MA 02215
> Research and intensive on-site management seminars for companies.

Work in America Institute, Inc.
700 White Plains Road
Scarsdale, NY 10583
914-472-9600
> A nonprofit organization that specializes in using human resources more efficiently in order to increase productivity.

Work/Family Initiatives
Beaver College
Glenside, PA 19038
215-572-2900
Research on balancing work and family.

Workplace Connections
200 Fifth Avenue
Waltham, MA 02154
617-890-5820
Consults with businesses to establish, from conception to implementation, parent-support programs for employees.

SOUTH CENTRAL

Career Dimensions
11520 North Central Expressway, Suite 141
Dallas, TX 75243
214-349-0573
Provides career counseling and assistance in developing flexible job schedules.

Creative Career Counseling
703 Shadywood Lane
Richardson, TX 75080
214-235-4689
Provides individual career counseling with an emphasis on alternative work schedules.

The Family Tree
605 W. St. Mary Boulevard
PO Box 2386
Lafayette, LA 70502
318-237-2164
Provides educational materials and conducts workshops for individuals and companies.

Rader, O'Neal, McGuinness & Co.
3200 Southwest Freeway, #2310
Houston, TX 77027
713-993-0847
  Placement firm for management-level temporaries.

SOUTHEAST

Career Resource
6845 Elm Street, Suite 710
McLean, VA 22101
703-821-3442
  Provides career counseling and workshops on stress management. Assists
  in the development of flexible work strategies.

Career Works Associates, Ltd.
1033 Quarrier Street, Suite 303
Charleston, WV 25301
304-344-2273
  Provides counseling and job-search workshops.

Institute for Women's Policy Research
1400 20th Street, N.W., Suite 104
Washington, DC 20036
202-785-5100
  Research on public policy issues regarding women and work.

KRON Medical Corp.
725 Airport Road, Suite 300
Chapel Hill, NC 27514
919-968-4881
  Temporary agency placing doctors.

Lawyer's Lawyer
1725 K Street, N.W.
Washington, DC 20006
202-362-3333
  Temporary or part-time legal placement firm.

Maryland New Directions, Inc.
2517 North Charles Street
Baltimore, MD 21218
301-235-8800
    Career counseling service providing assistance to individuals in transition.

Savants, Inc.
12 Norcross Street, Suite 200
Roswell, GA 30075
404-587-3234
    Placement firm for management-level temporaries.

Women's Bar Association
Part-Time Employment Exchange
8016 Hampton Lane
Bethesda, MD 20814
    Provides job bank for lawyers interested in less than full-time work.

Workplace Options
3344 Hillsborough Street
Raleigh, NC 27607
919-834-6506
    Provides companies with on-site seminars for working parents.

SOUTHWEST

Career Connections
PO Box 9331
Santa Fe, NM 87504-9331
505-983-9217
    Provides career counseling, job-search strategies, and assistance in negotiating flexible schedules.

Executive Staff Corp.
4411 Ace Kentucky Avenue
Denver, CO 30222
303-758-4966
> Placement firm for management-level temporaries.

Robert William James & Associates
2741 Mapleton Avenue
Boulder, CO 80304
303-443-1591
> Placement firm for management-level temporaries.

WEST/NORTHWEST

Career Action Center
445 Sherman Avenue
Palo Alto, CA 94306
415-324-1710 or 415-324-1715
> Nonprofit career development and employee resource center. Provides career counseling and flexible job-search strategies.

Career Targeting
1155 Filbert Street, #103
San Francisco, CA 94104
415-928-0707
> Specializes in flexible job schedules, outplacement, personnel guidelines, and recruiting.

The Corporate Staff
400 South El Camino Real, Suite 780
San Mateo, CA 94402
415-956-1202
> Placement firm for management-level temporaries.

Focus on Alternative Work Patterns
509 10th Avenue East
Seattle, WA 98102-5098
206-329-7918
  A membership organization that has a job clearinghouse for the Seattle area and works with employers and legislative staffs, advocating alternative work options.

The Lawsmiths
3388 24th Street
San Francisco, CA 94110
415-756-8555
  Temporary or part-time legal placement agency.

Linda Marks, Inc.
1177 Green Street
San Francisco, CA 94109
415-441-4520
  Consultant specializing in flexible work schedules.

Pace Network
PO Box 3386
Bellevue, WA 98009-3386
206-454-1075
  A placement firm specializing in job-sharing.

Parents in the Workforce
1838 El Camino Real, Suite 214
Burlingame, CA 94010
415-692-6647
  Provides consultation, employee surveys, and recommendations to employers on work/family programs. Also provide services to working parents through the employers.

Women at Work
78 North Marengo Avenue
Pasadena, CA 91101
818-796-6870
  Nonprofit community-based organization specializing in career development, balancing work and family, and flexible work schedules.

BIBLIOGRAPHY

"America's Mothers: Making It Work. How Women Balance the Demands of Jobs and Children." *Newsweek,* March 31, 1986.

"Balancing Work and Family: A Citizens' Agenda for the '90s." Roosevelt Center for American Policy Study, Washington, D.C., June 1989.

Berg, Barbara J., *The Crisis of the Working Mother.* Summit Books, New York, 1986.

Burden, Dianne S., Ph.D., and Bradley Googins, Ph.D., *Boston University Balancing Job and Homelife Study.* Boston University School of Social Work, Boston, 1987.

Christensen, Kathleen, Ph.D., "Flexible Staffing and Scheduling in U.S. Corporations." The Conference Board, New York, 1989.

———, *Women and Home-based Work: The Unspoken Contract.* Henry Holt and Co., New York, 1987.

Cohen, Herb, *You Can Negotiate Anything.* Bantam Books, New York, 1980.

Deutsch, Claudia H., "Getting Women Down to the Site." *New York Times,* March 11, 1990.

Ehrenreich, Barbara, and Deirdre English, *For Her Own Good: 150 Years of Experts' Advice to Women.* Doubleday, New York, 1979.

Evans, Sandra, "Area Parents Torn by Day Care Angst." *Washington Post,* August 3, 1989.

"Fertility of American Women: June 1988." U.S. Department of Commerce, Bureau of the Census, Series P-20, No. 436.

Finney, Martha I., "The ASPA Labor Shortage Survey." *Personnel Administrator,* February 1989.

231

Flexible Work Arrangements: Establishing Options For Managers and Professionals, 1989. Available from Catalyst, 250 Park Ave. South, New York, NY 10003.

Flexible Workstyles: A Look at Contingent Labor. U.S. Department of Labor, Women's Bureau, 1988.

Friedan, Betty, *The Second Stage.* Summit Books, New York, 1981.

Friedman, Dana E., "Work vs. Family: War of the Worlds." *Personnel Administrator,* August 1987.

Galinsky, Ellen, "Child Care and Productivity." Families and Work Institute, New York, 1988.

———, "Family Life and Corporate Policies." Families and Work Institute, New York, 1986.

———, "Labor Force Participation of Dual-Earner Couples and Single Parents." Families and Work Institute, New York, 1989.

———, "The Impact of Supervisors' Attitudes and Company Culture on Work/Family Adjustment." Families and Work Institute, New York, 1988.

———, "The Implementation of Flexible Time and Leave Policies: Observations from European Employers." Families and Work Institute, New York, 1989.

———, and Diane Hughes, "The *Fortune* Magazine Child Care Study." Families and Work Institute, New York, 1987.

———, Diane Hughes, and Judy David, "Trends in Corporate Family-Responsive Policies." Families and Work Institute, New York, 1988.

The General Mills American Family Report: 1980–81. Conducted by Louis Harris and Associates, Inc., for General Mills, Minneapolis, 1981.

Genevie, Louis, Ph.D., and Eva Margolies, *The Motherhood Report: How Women Feel About Being Mothers.* Macmillan Publishing, New York, 1987.

Hennig, Margaret, and Anne Jardim, *The Managerial Woman.* Pocket Books, New York, 1977.

Hewlett, Sylvia Ann, *A Lesser Life.* William Morrow & Co., New York, 1986.

Hochschild, Arlie, *The Second Shift.* Viking, New York, 1989.

Hooks, Karen L., "Alternative Work Schedules and the Woman CPA." American Society of Certified Public Accountants, September 1989.

Houff, James N., and William J. Wiatrowski, "Analyzing Short-term Disability Benefits." *Monthly Labor Review,* June 1989.

Hughes, Diane, and Ellen Galinsky, "Balancing Work and Family Life: Research and Corporate Application." Familes and Work Institute, New York, 1988.

Indexed Bibliography of Alternative Work Schedules. Available from Catalyst, 250 Park Ave. South, New York, NY 10003.

Johnston, William B., and Arnold H. Packer, *Workforce 2000: Work and Workers for the 21st Century.* Hudson Institute, Indianapolis, June 1987.

Kamerman, Sheila B., and Cheryl D. Hayes, eds., *Families that Work: Children in a Changing World.* National Academy Press, Washington, D.C., 1982.

———, Alfred J. Kahn, and Paul Kingston, *Maternity Policies and Working Women.* Columbia University Press, New York, 1983.

Karen, Robert, "Becoming Attached: What Children Need." *The Atlantic,* February 1990.

Kilborn, Peter T., "Milwaukee Helps Pace U.S. as Innovator for Workplace." *New York Times,* October 12, 1989.

Kolbe, Kathy, *The Conative Connection.* Addison-Wesley, New York, 1990.

Lawson, Carol, "7 Employers Join to Provide Child Care at Home in a Crisis." *New York Times,* September 7, 1989.

McBroom, Patricia A., *The Third Sex: The New Professional Women.* William Morrow & Co., New York, 1986.

Magid, Renee Y., with Nancy F. Fleming, *When Mothers and Fathers Work.* Avon, New York, 1987.

"Management Women: Debating the Facts of Life." Letters to the Editor, *Harvard Business Review,* May–June 1989.

"Medical and Family Leave Benefits Available to Female Workers in the United States." NCJW Center for the Child, National Council of Jewish Women, New York, March 1987.

Morin, Richard, "National Poll Finds Support for Day Care as Employee Benefit." *Washington Post,* September 3, 1989.

"Mothers in the Workplace Working Paper: The Role of Managers/Supervisors in Easing Work-Family Strain." National Council of Jewish Women, December 1988.

Naisbitt, John, and Patricia Aburdeen, *Megatrends 2000.* William Morrow & Co., New York, 1990.

Nierenberg, Gerald I., *The Art of Negotiating.* Pocket Books, New York, 1981.

"1989 AMS Flexible Work Survey," Administrative Management Society. Trevose, PA, 1989.

Olmstead, Barney, and Suzanne Smith, *Creating a Flexible Workplace: How to Select and Manage Alternative Work Options.* American Management Association, New York, 1989.

"Onward, Women!" *Time,* December 4, 1989.

Quindlen, Anna, "Truth in Child Care." Editorial Page, *New York Times,* March 18, 1990.

Rodgers, Fran Sussner, and Charles Rodgers, "Business and the Facts of Family Life. *Harvard Business Review,* Nov.–Dec. 1989.

Schwartz, Felice N., "Management Women and the New Facts of Life." *Harvard Business Review,* Jan.–Feb. 1989.

Sidel, Ruth, *Women and Children Last.* Viking Press, New York, 1986.

Skrzycki, Cindy, "Family Concerns Spark Changes at Work. *Washington Post,* August 3, 1989, page 1.

Teltsch, Kathleen, "For Younger and Older, Workplace Day Care." *New York Times,* March 10, 1990.

The American Woman 1990–91: A Status Report. Women's Research and Education Institute, W. W. Norton & Co., New York, 1990.

"The Day Care Generation." *Special Edition: The 21st Century Family, Newsweek,* Winter/Spring 1990.

"The 30 Best Companies for Working Mothers." *Working Mother,* August 1986.

"The 40 Best Companies in America for Working Mothers." *Working Mother,* August 1987.

"The 50 Best Companies for Working Mothers." *Working Mother,* October 1988.

"The 60 Best Companies for Working Mothers." *Working Mother,* October 1989.

VandenHeuvel, Audrey, "The Sequencing of Roles: Mothers' Life-Course Patterns After First Birth." Doctoral dissertation, University of North Carolina, Chapel Hill, 1989.

Washington Post Child Care Poll, Summary of Results. June 1989 (unpublished).

"What Happened to the Family?" *Special Edition: The 21st Century Family, Newsweek,* Winter/Spring 1990.

"Who's Minding the Kids." U.S. Department of Commerce, Bureau of the Census, Series P-70, #9, May 1987.

"Work and Family: Combining Commitments." *Personnel Administrator,* Special Issue, August 1987.

Work and Family Issues. Personnel Administrator, Reprint Collection Series, American Society for Personnel Administration, Alexandria, VA.

"Work and Family Programs: A Growing Benefit for Small Companies." BNA Special Report Series on Work and Family, Special Report #25, Bureau of National Affairs, Washington, D.C. 1990.

Work and Family Responsibilities: Achieving a Balance. Ford Foundation, March 1989.

Yankelovitch, Clancy Shulman, "Findings from *Time*/CNN Poll of American Women." Unpublished memo, December 1, 1989.

Zeitz, Baila, Ph.D., and Lorraine Dusky, *The Best Companies for Women.* Pocket Books, New York, 1988.

Zigler, Edward F., and Meryl Frank, eds., *The Parental Leave Crisis: Toward a National Policy.* Yale University Press, New Haven, 1988.

INDEX

Absenteeism, family care as reason
   for, 13, 22–23, 124
Accountemps/Robert Half Interna-
   tional, 213
Accounting firms, and flexibility,
   78, 82–83
Administrative Management Soci-
   ety, 220
Adoption aid, 71
Aetna Life & Casualty, 37, 45, 47,
   54, 56, 60, 74, 156, 190
Ainsworth, Mary, 70
Allstate Insurance Co., 74
Alternatrack, 107, 220
American Bankers Insurance
   Group, 41
American Cyanamid Co., 74
American Express, 41–42, 44, 49,
   51, 60, 74, 190–91
American Greetings Corp., 74
American Information Technologies
   Corporation (Ameritech),
   74

American Woman's Society of Cer-
   tified Public Accountants
   (AWSCPA), 82
Apple Computer, 39, 45, 49, 53,
   54, 57, 114
Arthur Andersen, 51, 74, 82–83,
   191–92
Associates, communicating with,
   156
Association of Part-Time Profes-
   sionals (APTP), 106–7,
   213, 220
Atkins, George, 106
Attachment theory, 70–71
Attitude, and flexibility, 84

Backup system, creating, 159–60
Baker, Jane, 126
Bausch & Lomb, 56, 192
Beary, Bianca, 183
Beeby, Thomas, 79
B.E.&K., Inc., 12
Belsky, Jay, 71

Benefits
  and contract workers, 86–87
  and flexibility, 128–29
  and part-time workers, 60
Best Western International, 105
Beth Israel Hospital of Boston, 57
Better Way, Inc., Strategies, 218
Bevins, Sandy, 109
Billings, Mary, 17–18, 22
Biondolillo, Deborah, 53, 114–15
Black, Anita, 103–4
Black, Barbara, 166–67
Blake, Wendy, 179
Bollinger, Madeline, 172
Boston University Job and Home-
    life Study, 21, 45
Bowman, Carolyn, 138
Brazelton, T. Berry, M.D., 70
Brescia, Marian, 26
Brodie, Carolyn, 157
Brown, Mike, 202
Burden, Dianne, 21
Bureau of National Affairs, 214
Burlington, Hannah, 175, 176
Burlington, Peter, 175
Buxton, Julieanne, 182–83

California Child Care Initiative, 12
Campbell, Jean, 36–37
Campbell Soup, 39
Career Action Center, 228
Career Connections, 227
Career Development Services, 221
Career Dimensions, 225
Career Resource, 226
Careers Unlimited, 221
Career Targeting, 228
Career Transition Resources, 221
Career Works Associates, Ltd., 226
Casper, Pat Quinn, 149–52, 168–
    69
Catalyst, 58, 65, 69, 73, 74, 75, 83,
    112, 125, 214
Center for Parenting Studies, 221
Center for Research and Education
    in the Workplace, 221

Champion International, 63
Child care, 22–24
  company programs in, 12–13,
    41–42, 44
  consistency as problem in, 22–23
  effect of, on children, 23–24
  flexibility in, 102
  initiatives, 44
  lack of available, 11
  myth about, 178
  as not just women's issue, 10–14
  parents on, 23
  quality as problem in, 23–24
  resource and referral, 40
  role of father in, 21
  sick, 42
  on-site, 39
  and stress, 23, 25–26, 41
  and telecommuting, 77, 178
Christensen, Kathleen, 31, 58, 177
Cinderella Complex, 18
Clark, Colleen, 142–44, 185
Clarke, Sarah, 4–5, 6
Clearinghouse on Work and Family,
    214
Clients, communicating with, 156
Colgate-Palmolive, 12
College graduates, decline in, 32
Collins, Jane, 62–63, 64
Communication, and job flexibility,
    127–28
Community life, and job flexibility,
    183
Compressed work week, 41, 209
Conference Board Inc., 214
Conover, Ann, 172
Conover, Kate, 176
Contingent labor force, 28
Contract workers, 86–87
Conway, Elizabeth, 162
Cook, Karen, 107
Corning, Inc., 38, 54, 56, 59, 192–
    93
Corporate culture
  assessing, 113–15
  new facts of, 34–37

Corporate policies, 45
Corporate Staff, 228
Co-workers, explaining your ar-
    rangement to, 155–56
Crawford, Cathy, 3–4, 6, 30
Creative Career Counseling, 225

Daddy track, 47, 78–80
Dail, Hilda Lee, & Associates, In-
    ternational, 222
Davis, Nadine, 23–24
Day care. See Child care
Day-care workers, turnover rates
    for, 22
Deeken, Hanneke, 149–52, 168
Delta Air Lines, Inc., 74
Deluxe Corp., 74
Demographics, 124
Dials, Jennifer, 172
Digital Equipment Corp., 46, 54,
    56, 74, 193–94
Dillon, Mike, 143
Disability leave program, 54
Discrimination, and flexible jobs,
    85–86
Dorsey, Madeline, 118
Dow Chemical, 45, 74
DuPont, 9, 23, 43–44, 44, 45, 57,
    74
Durbin, Kendall, 163
Dynerman, Susan, 8–10, 34, 67,
    100, 164–65

Eastman Kodak, 53, 56, 74, 194
Easton, Jane, 186
Economics, of job flexibility, 174–
    81
Ego, impact of loss of status on,
    101
Elkins, Glenda, 5–6, 30
Elwood, Susan, 97
Employee Assistance Programs
    (EAPs), 49
Employer
    finding job flexibility with cur-
        rent, 112–13

as source of flexible employment,
    105
Englund, Will, 79
Equality, women's interest in, 84–
    89
Equity issue, 59
Ernst & Young, 12
Errigo, D. Donald, 192
Evans, Sally, 98
Ewing, Margo, 138–40
Executive Corner, 221
Executive Staff Corp., 228
Experts, 222
Extended work week, 209
Exxon Corp., 74

Family, and job flexibility, 184
Families and Work Institute, 39, 40,
    58, 215
Family Resource Coalition, 215
Family Service America, 215
Family Tree, 225
Farrell, Celia, 125
Federal Trade Commission (FTC),
    parental leave policy, 132
Fel-Pro, 57, 58–59
Fino, Raymond, 207
Fitzpatrick, Linda, 54
Flexdays, 45
Flexibility. See Job flexibility
Flexible schedule
    definition of, 209
    managing on a, 162–63
Flexteam (Du Pont), 45
Flextime, 27–28, 41
    availability of, 63
    definition of, 209
Floodgate issue, 59
Focus on Alternative Work Patterns,
    229
Former employer as source of flexi-
    ble employment, 106
Four-day week, 26
Frank, Meryl, 77
Fraser, Jean, 49
Freedman, Johanna, 21

Freelancers Over 50, 222
Freilvogel, Margaret, 79
Freilvogel, William, 79
Friedan, Betty, 10
Friedman, Eleanor, 147–49
Friends, and job flexibility, 184–85

Galinsky, Ellen, 13, 15, 39
Gannett Co., Inc., 74
Genentech, Inc., 54
Gilday, Sarah, 110
Gil Gordon Associates, 215
Gochman, Eileen, 40
Goldsborough, Sarah, 165
Goodmeasure, Inc., 125
Googins, Bradley, 21
Gordon, Gil, 31
Government, flexible employment
  in, 62–66, 107–8
Goya, Donna, 199
Graham, Marcy, 185
Griffin, Becky, 136–38
Griffin, Sean, 136–38
Group 243, 57
Guilt, 20

Haas, Bob, 200
Hall, Deborah, 107
Hallmark Cards, Inc., 74
Handy, Liza, 171
Harvey, Derek, 35, 37
Hayes, Lynn, 8–10, 95, 98–100,
  104, 164–65
Hayes, Nancy, 160
Hazard, Bob, 157
Hazelton, Cindy, 95–96
Hechinger Co., 74
Heldenberg, Ann, 105–6
Henderson, June, 179
Herchenroether, Sherry, 37, 47, 59,
  190
Herman Miller, Inc., 74
Hevey, Dorothy, 78
Hewitt Associates, 12–13, 49, 83
Hewlett-Packard, 54, 74, 195–96
Hidden job market, 104

Hochschild, Arlie, 20, 174–75
Hoffman-La Roche, 39, 196
Home-based work, 41
Home Box Office, 57
Honeycutt, Jan, 75
Honeywell, Inc., 45, 54, 74, 197
Hoogerhyde, Peggy, 145–47, 172
Housework, 20
  male participation in, 20, 21–22,
  48, 177–78
Howes, Carollee, 22

Illinois Bell, 39
Improved relationships, and job
  flexibility, 183–84
Innovation, turning into income,
  125
Institute for Women and Work, 222
Institute for Women's Policy Re-
  search, 226
Interim Management Corp., 222
International Business Machines
  (IBM), 9, 44, 51, 57, 73–
  74, 124, 197–98

Jackson, Lisa, 130
Job, redefining, 117–18
Job counseling and placement services, 36
Job flexibility, 77
  and attitude, 84
  business reasons for, 29–33
  and community life, 183
  and daddy track, 78–80
  economics of, 174–81
  emergence as major issue, 43–44
  and equality, 84–89
  facing reality, 100–3
  finding with your current employer, 112–13
  formalizing, 53–54
  in government, 62–66
  and improved relationships,
  183–84
  increases in, 52–53

job-sharing, 27, 41, 138–40,
145–47, 149–52, 163–69
and keeping your foot in the
door, 185
leaders in, 51–66
learning to say no, 157–59
and lifestyles, 80
part-time, 136–38
payoffs in, 182
pitfalls in, 180
and professional track, 80–84
and promotability, 171–73
quest for, 46–50
and recruiting, 77–78
resistance to, 59–60
and retraining, 80
scaling back on work hours, 96–
100
searching job, 103–8
shifting hours, 134–35
shortened hours, 134–35, 140–
42, 147–49, 152–53
as social issue, 14–16
sources of information for,
104–8
steps in making work, 121–23,
154–57
and productivity, 155, 160–61
communicating with clients/as-
sociates, 156
communicating with supervisor, 155
creating backup system, 159–
60
explaining arrangement to co-
workers, 155–56
managing schedule, 162–63
renegotiating plans, 157
securing management support,
154–55
taking advantage of training,
156
and stress, 182–83
strategies for, 131–53
telecommuting, 27, 31, 65, 136–
38, 142–44, 169–71

and time, 125–26, 181–82,
185–86
and your family, 184
and your friends, 184–85
and your spouse, 184
Job-sharers, relationship between,
180
Job-sharing, 8–10, 27, 41, 138–40,
145–47, 149–52, 163–64
and advancement, 83
and attitude, 61–62
benefitting from, 164–67
and communication, 102
definition of, 210
facts on, 61
for management position, 168–
69
strategy for, 138–40
working out the details, 167–68
Johnson, Arlene, 7, 36, 41, 88,
116
Johnson, Howard, 195
Johnson & Johnson, 39, 42–43,
46, 48, 54, 74, 76, 198–99
Joice, Wendell, 64
Journalism, job sharing in, 79–80

Kantor, Rosabeth Moss, 125
Karen, Robert, 70–71
Karol Rose, 205
Keeping your foot in the door, and
job flexibility, 185
Kipp, Michael, 94
Kjeldsen, Chris, 42, 46, 199
Klavens, Cecile, 61, 62
Kleinman, Marcia, 100
Klivans, Becker & Smith, 219
Knight-Ridder, Inc., 74
Kolbe, Kathy, 160–61
Koppel, Ted, 10
Kramer, Quinn, 54
Kraus, George, 93
KRON Medical Corp., 226
Kyl, Cherie, 128

Labor force
changing needs of a changing, 17–33
contingent, 28
growth of, 32
minorities in, 33
new mothers in, 69
women in, 15–16, 33
Lally, Kathy, 79
Landon, Lucia, 219
Lang, Susan, 101
Lange, Molly, 166–67
Latchkey kids, 24–26
Law firms, and flexibility, 80–82
Lawsmiths, 229
Lawson, Roger, 62–63, 64
Lawyer's Lawyer, 226
Leave. *See also* Maternity leave; Parental leave
definition of, 210
Levi Strauss & Co., 37–38, 39, 45, 56, 199–200
Lifestylers, 80
Linda Marks, Inc., 229
Lockheed Corp., 74
Loyalty, 124

Madden, Molly, 128
Madison, Nancy, 152–53
Malloy, Eileen, 134–35
Malloy, Ellen, 97
Management Assistance Group, 223
Management consulting firms, and flexibility, 83–84
Management support, securing, 154–55
Management training, 49
Manufacturers Hanover, 61
Margolies, Laurie, 46
Markey, Mary, 158
Marks, Linda, 104, 175
Marriott Corporation, 37, 45, 48
Maryland New Directions, Inc., 227
Mason, Ann, 184

Maternity leave, 67–74. *See also* Parental leave
creative solutions for, 75–77
and part-time return option, 74
and telecommuting, 77
Maternity Protection Recommendation, 72
Maxwell, Mary Ann, 184
McGraw-Hill, Inc., 74
McMillan, Carolyn, 106
Men
home responsibilities of, 20, 21–22, 48, 177–78
interest of, in job flexibility, 43–44
and parental leave program, 48–49
and telecommuting, 65
Merck & Co., 51, 53, 57–58, 74, 200
Metropolitan Life Insurance Co., 74
Miller, Herman, Inc., 194–95
Minnesota Mining & Manufacturing Co. (3M), 74, 200
Minnesota Work and Family Institute, 219
Mitchell, Terri, 94–95
Mobil Corp., 35, 36, 37, 74
"Mommy Track," 9–10, 80, 171
Moore, Ann, 75–76
Moore, Suzanne Renfrit, 107
Morale, improved, 124–25
Morazza, Barbara, 177
Morris, Richard, 59
Morrison & Foerster, 57, 81, 201–2
Mosley, Sherry, 38–39, 193
Motherhood Report, 20
Mothers, new, in the work force, 69
Mullan, Lisa, 203

Nappi, Karen, 30
National Association For Women in Careers, 216

National Council for Research on Women, 216
National Council of Jewish Women, 72, 116, 216
National Council of Jewish Women Center for the Child, 69–70, 72
National Project for Homed-Based Work, 58
Nealon, Judy, 93
Negotiating, 109–11
  assessing corporate culture, 113–15
  benefits, 128–29
  closing deal, 129–30
  decision making, 115–17
  finding right words, 127–28
  fuel for arguments, 124–25
  guidelines for effective, 110–11
  job flexibility with current employer, 112–13
  redefining your job, 117–18
  steps toward flexibility, 121–23
  timing, 125–26
  work units, 118–21
Nelson, Judy, 105
New Ways to Work, 48, 58, 62, 216
Niles, Liza, 117
9 to 5, 216
No, learning to say, 157–59
Northeast Utilities, 56, 59, 202
Nynex Corp., 74

Of Counsel Inc., 219
Olmsted, Barney, 47, 48, 62, 80
On-site child care, 39
Operation Able of Greater Boston, 223
Option Research Corp., 40
Options, Inc., 100, 223

Pace Network, 229
Pacific Gas & Electric Co., 74
Pacific Telesis Group, 74
Paperman, Dan, 96
Parent Action, 217

Parental leave. *See also* Maternity leave
  getting information on, 77
  policies on, 48–49, 54
  strategies for, 37
Parents in the Workforce, 229
Parker, Jane, 85–86
Partnership Group, 223
Part-time work, 28–29, 41
  definition of, 210
  and health benefits, 60
  makeup of workforce in, 54–55
  myths on, 87
  and retraining, 80
  as return option, 69, 73, 74
Paynes, Nicole, 25
Pearce, Joe, 59
Penney, J. C., 156
Personal time off, 45
Personnel Projects, 219
Pesce, Peter, 83
Phased retirement, 41
Philips, Jane, 185
Pickwick Group, 61, 223
Pioneer Hi-Bred International, Inc., 56, 203
Placement services, for flexible work arrangements, 107
Princeton Entrepreneurial Resources, 223
Procter & Gamble, 57, 124
Productivity, 124, 155, 160–61
Project on Home-Based Work, 217
Promotability, 171–73
Public Relations Society of America (PRSA), 107

Quality International, 98
Quindlen, Anna, 23

Rader, O'Neal, McGuinness & Co., 226
Raymond, Pamela, 158
Reality, facing, 100–3
Recruiting, 77–78, 124
Reduced work schedules, 38–39

Relocation, unwillingness to, 35–37
Replacement costs, 124
Resources, guide to, 213–29
Resources for Child Care Management, 217
Resources for Parents at Work, 224
Retraining, 80
Rifkin, Ellen, 41
Robert Half International, 14
Robert William James & Associates, 228
Roberts, Rennie, 42, 191
Rodgers, Fran, 68–69, 88, 113
Roosevelt Center for American Policy Studies, 217
Rose, Kate, 131–34
Rosenthal, Jane, 26

Saliers, Ann, 145–47, 172
San Francisco Bay Area Child Care Coalition, 202
Santamour, Melissa, 118–21
SAS Institute, Inc., 39, 57
Savants, Inc., 227
Schwartz, Felice, 9
Scordato, Christine, 102
Sears, Roebuck and Co., 74
Self-employment, women in, 30–31
Shortened hours, 96–100, 134–35, 140–42, 147–49, 152–53, 210
Simmons, Jan, 93–94
Skadden Arps Slate Meagher & Flom, 12
Skinner, Patty, 101–2
Smith, Suzanne, 62
Spouse, and job flexibility, 184
Staff Alternative, 224
Staggered hours, 210
Staines, Graham, 28
Steelcase, Inc., 51, 54, 56, 59, 124, 156, 203–4
Stephens, Janet, 115

Stillman, Andrea, 101
Stress
  and child care, 23, 25–26, 41
  and job flexibility, 182–83
  for the working woman, 20
Stride Rite, 39
Sullivan, Mary, 128
Supervisor, communicating with, 155
Superwomen myth, 18–19
Susanne Parente Associates, Inc., 224
Syntex, 57

Telecommuting, 27, 31, 65, 136–38, 142–44, 169–70
  and child care, 77, 178
  definition of, 211
  motivations behind, 65
  temporary, 75
  working out the details, 170–71
Textron, Inc., 74
Thurgood, Marcia, 86
Time, and job flexibility, 125–26, 181–82, 185–86
Time, Inc., 12, 51, 74, 75, 156, 204–5
Time banks, 45
Tompkins, Richard, 115–16
Trainer, Nancy, 112
Training, take advantage of, 156
Travelers Insurance, 74, 205–6
Tuition assistance, 76
Turnover, reduced, 124
Two-income families, 14–15
  and relocation, 35–37
Type A personality, and job flexibility, 180

Urban, Tom, 203
U.S. Government Office of Personnel Management, 217
US Sprint, 36, 45, 53, 74, 206
US West, Inc., 44, 56, 59, 74, 76, 117, 156, 206–7

VandenHeuvel, Audrey, 31–32
Vellinga, Dee, 207
Vera Sullivan Associates, 224
Voice mail system, 53

Wade, Marie, 159–60
Warner-Lambert Co., 74, 207–8
Wellesley College Center for Research on Women, 218
Wheelock College Center for Parenting Studies, 224
Wille, Dave, 83
Wohl, Faith, 43
Wolf, Nancy, 27
Women
  and equality issue, 84–89
  in labor force, 15–16, 33
  and need for flexibility, 10–14
  in self-employment, 30–31
  working, and stress, 20
Women at Work, 229
Women Employed Institute, 219
Women's Bar Association, 107, 227
Woodside, Sharon, 140–42
Work and Family Information Center, 7, 36
Work and Family Life Seminar Program, 218
Work and Family Resources, 218
Work and Family Spectrum, 220
Work/family agenda, 37–50
  adoption aid, 71
  child care, 40, 41–43, 45, 49
  Employee Assistance Programs (EAPS), 49

flexibility, 43, 46–50
  parental leave strategies, 37, 45
  personal time off, 45
  reduced work schedules, 38–39
  relocation, 37
Work/Family Directions, Inc., 36, 68, 218
Work/Family Initiatives, 225
Work/family programs
  change in, 45
  publicity value of, 51
Workforce 2000, 32
Work hours, scaling back on, 96–100, 134–35, 140–42, 147–49, 152–53
Work in America Institute, Inc., 224
Working Parent Resource Center, 220
Working women
  bias against, 22
  and guilt, 20
  realities for, 17–29
  reasons for, 88–89
  and stress, 20
Workplace, reshaping of, 34–50
Workplace Connections, 225
Workplace Options, 227
Work units, 118–21

Xerox Corp., 74

Young, Allison, 126

Zigler, Edward F., 77